Take Heart

Take Heart

Rosalie Givens Alderman

Broadman Press
Nashville, Tennessee

4255–34

ISBN: 0–8054–5534–5

Dewey Decimal Classification: 248.4

Subject heading: CHRISTIAN SOCIAL MINISTRIES

Library of Congress Catalog Card Number: 78–59782

Printed in the United States of America

Dedicated to:

The residents of Heritage Manor Nursing Home in Hope, Arkansas, who are gripping testimonies to the miracles that can still be wrought by the ill and the elderly who sing the Lord's song (by their works) in their own particular "strange lands."

The staff members who care deeply for them as people, not as mere "residents." Their genuine welcome each time they see me makes my going to the home a pleasure.

Dr. Lowell Harris, whose treatment during the first years of my illness aided in my recovery. His exhortation "Remember your faith in God" inspired me to do even the little that I could do at the time and led finally to my hearing and accepting God's call to this rewarding work.

Dr. J. W. Branch, Sr., owner of the nursing home and my present physician. The appreciation he regularly expresses to all the volunteers on our team helps us to not only do our best but to enjoy doing so.

My husband, Edwin, whose hard work provides me with a good car and enough money for the gasoline needed to be about the work each day. He often encourages me by expressing his respect for the work I do.

Finally, and most important, to Jesus Christ, who saw fit to call me to this ministry and to enable me to continue in it.

Acknowledgments

Dr. Erwin L. McDonald, while editor of *Arkansas Baptist News-magazine,* learned of the Heritage Manor ministry and requested that I write an article on the work. After publishing it, he insisted that the courage of the Heritage Manor residents who rose to the challenge to "work until the last breath is drawn" was a thrilling witness which should be told in book form. But except for his friendship and his beyond-the-line-of-duty encouragement, I would not have written it. I was so busy *doing* the work that it seemed impossible to also write about it. I am grateful to Dr. McDonald for convincing me that the "fruit" of the book might be similar ministries in other nursing homes. To that end it was written.

Dr. Joe T. Odle, editor of the *Baptist Record* in Mississippi, and my husband, Edwin, read the manuscript and made suggestions for its improvement. Dr. McDonald also helped in this capacity.

Mrs. W. H. Peterson, Jr. (Dorcas) assisted me in typing its original pages; and my sister, Mrs. Lucille Radford, typed the final manuscript.

Another inestimable help has been the faithful prayers of the folks at Heritage Manor for "Teacher" as "our book" was being written. Their term, "our book," helped to keep "Teacher" at the task when the temptation to give it all up was especially hard to resist.

Foreword

"God blessed me with a heart attack!"

"Blessed?" "With a heart attack?"

Strange words. Yet they are the message the reader hears Rosalie Alderman communicating.

This is the story of a heart attack that proved to be a blessing—not just to the one who experienced it, but to a host of other people as well.

How could this be? Everybody knows that a heart attack is not a blessing.

God did it!

A heart attack halted Mrs. Alderman's many activities. This brought about a slowdown that led to her eyes being opened and seeing people she never had seen before.

Having to sit quietly and to take a new view of life led to a discovery most of us have not made. Maybe we too need to be slowed down from the fast pace of life so that we can find time to look around us.

Mrs. Alderman did that; and she discovered people, lonely people, hundreds of them. They were all around her, but never had she seen them before—at least, not as she began to see them after her heart attack.

The people she saw are all around all of us: in every city, in every town, in every village, and in every rural area.

Most of us, however, are so busy that we are hardly aware of their presence. Others of us know about them; but we are prone to forget, or even purposely do so, because they disturb our consciences. We do not want to be bothered.

Mrs. Alderman, however, had to stop. Her heart demanded it. And while she was stopped, God opened her eyes and said,

"Look!" When she did she saw people.

Who are these people?

They are the aged, the ill, the blind, the shut-ins. Mostly they are those whose age has brought infirmities and sometimes illness. Some have broken health and even disordered minds.

Many are in small cottages or tiny apartments where they are barely able to subsist on small incomes and minimal care. Others are in nursing homes, which have been developed to help care for the increasing number of senior citizens needing some care.

Some of these homes are modern facilities, built to meet the highest standards for such care. Others are little more than old dwellings with added halls and rooms, set up to meet the minimal standards necessary to collect a fee for giving care to the aged.

When one visits these homes he finds all types of people. There are those who have come out of deep poverty and those who have enjoyed the better things of life. There are those with little education and those who have achieved the highest places in the cultural world. Here are people who have been teachers, business people, farmers, professional men and women, and people from other walks of life. Now their days of active service are gone. Pain may rack their bodies and loneliness chill their hearts. Sometimes they lie on their beds, unable to get up. At other times they are in wheelchairs. Some have good enough health that they can walk with their canes or walkers or even move up and down the halls unassisted. Sometimes they watch television, and sometimes they just sit and stare into space as if living with their memories.

Here they are—lonely, needy, often frustrated people. Does anybody care? Yes, some care. Loved ones, husbands or wives, sons or daughters, grandchildren, or brothers or sisters come regularly to visit or to minister to their needs.

Others have friends or old acquaintances who have not forgotten them and who come to bring words and gifts of love and cheer. There are church groups—pastors, deacons, teachers, church visitors, youth groups, choirs, and others who come to hold services, to bring literature and to visit, thus bringing spiritual ministry to these who likely can no longer attend church. There are civic groups, community clubs, and other individuals who come simply because they want to minister to people who need them.

Thankfully, government agencies are also taking an interest in care for the aged. Meals for shut-ins, minibus service, daily telephone calls, nursing visits, and similar activities are all meaning much, especially to those who live alone or to couples who are confined to their homes. Of course, almost all of these older people are under the care of dedicated doctors, and those in nursing homes are watched over by nurses and aides.

Yet all of these ministries may lack the depth of meaning that spiritually led, personal service of Christian love can give. When Christian individuals, motivated by the Holy Spirit, reach out to people in the name of Christ, heavenly things begin to happen. This book tells of a person who heard God's call to be concerned for such people. Out of this call has grown a service that is both highly beautiful and deeply meaningful.

Rosalie Alderman did not choose a ministry to lonely people in nursing homes as an area of service that had a special appeal for her. Rather, God almost pressed her into it. As he did, she came to understand how his direction of her life gave her a special preparation for the task before her. Her story is a fascinating and intriguing record of what one person can do—and can inspire others to do—when he or she ministers to others in the name of Christ. It shows how sunshine and joy, love and hope come into the hearts and lives of many people when such ministry develops.

You will rejoice as you feel the warm response of lonely hearts; you will feel the stirring of the Spirit as you see how he can use us. You will weep as you feel the heartbeat of people, especially as you walk with "Teacher" through the deep waters that prepared her for this ministry.

And as you read these pages you may be inspired and challenged to try to do something about the lonely and needy people who are all around you.

I have known Rosalie Alderman for many years, for a few as her pastor and for many more as a friend. As I have read her story, it has sent thrills through my heart. And I know it will do the same for all who read it. It is a human story, about real people, and presents vibrant life.

The book is a testimony of what God has been able to do with one person who caught the vision of God's will for her special ministry. "The Lord's song" will sound in other "strange lands." And what a blessing that will bring to the world when it happens.

JOE T. ODLE

Jackson, Mississippi

Introduction

When Rosalie Givens Alderman was a child she was enthralled by the song "Dixie." One day she told her mother that she hoped sometime to go and see Dixieland. "Honey, you've never been anywhere else!" replied her mother, referring to their native south Mississippi.

Just as she was in Dixieland and didn't realize it, many people are in their land of opportunity to work for God but have not yet recognized it, she reminds her readers.

Take Heart is well named. It holds out hope for the despondent and rest for the weary. Its inspiration is matched only by its good humor and down-to-earth practicality. Here is a rare workbook for Christians interested in serving on one of the greatest mission fields of the land—the nursing homes.

ERWIN L. McDONALD
Editor Emeritus, Arkansas Baptist Newsmagazine

My Rehabilitated Life

By a nursing home resident

Seven years ago I was a man who no longer even hoped for a time when my life would again have meaning. Any thought of rehabilitation would have seemed but an empty dream.

I was embittered by disappointments, depressed by the loss of health, and unsure as to whether I had a saving faith in Jesus Christ.

The first step in my rehabilitation was my sister, Mrs. Cathryn Tedder. She stood by me through all the years of my trouble. When I expressed a desire to leave the nursing home where I had been for some time, she brought me to Heritage Manor to look the place over.

I chose to stay, and I feel that the choice was the next step toward my changed outlook on life. I am convinced that God was directing my path. At the time, though, I was so disillusioned with life that I did not believe God had any interest in me.

A day or so later I met Rosalie Alderman. She had begun teaching a Wednesday morning Bible class for the residents two weeks before my arrival. Both she and Mrs. Pauline Frazier, supervisor at the time, encouraged me to attend.

I did so but with reluctance. I expected to be bored by hearing a lot of nonsense about how God would comfort us "poor sick folks who were unable to work."

I was mistaken in that.

She taught from the twenty-fifth chapter of Matthew. Not as though it all concerned "somebody, somewhere." We could see *ourselves* as the ones whose talents God expected to be used for him. We realized that the Lord would say to *us*, "Thou good and faithful servant . . . enter thou into the joy of thy Lord."

Or he might say, "Inasmuch as ye did it *not* to one of the least of these, ye did it not to me."

I was impressed but would not join in the singing or quote a Bible verse as the other residents did.

A day or so later the teacher visited me. She tried to encourage me by telling me what God would do for me if I would only let him. I was impressed by what she said and by her sincerity. But I was so depressed that I still took no part in the services except to attend.

Her husband came and taught us one day when she could not be with us. I was impressed by him. He began taking me out to their farm, where I enjoyed watching the animals and breathing the fresh air. This meant more to me than it's possible to explain, as it helped me regain my feeling of dignity as a man. Only God knows how lonely a sick man can get for another man to treat him as an equal.

I began finally to join in the singing but would not quote a Bible verse.

The teacher kept coming to see me and encouraging me. Mrs. Mae Bell Revis had become supervisor, and she too encouraged me.

When Mrs. Alderman invited me to attend church with her and her husband, I was skeptical. Others had promised to take me but never did so. So I asked, "Do you mean it?" "Yes," she answered, "we will pick you up shortly after nine o'clock Sunday morning." I still attend Sunday School and church with them every Sunday.

I talked to Mrs. Alderman about joining the church and being baptized. I also talked to Brother Trussell, a wonderful man and a good pastor. I accepted the Lord and was baptized.

Soon afterward Mrs. Alderman and the others who had by then joined her in the work asked me to be their chaplain in residence. I prayed about the matter and reluctantly accepted the responsibility. That was in 1972. I am still serving in that capacity and am gratified by the hope that my work is of some help to the others in the home.

My teacher's untiring efforts and her husband's interest in me have blessed and helped me more than I can say. Others have helped in my partial recovery—Mrs. Revis, Mrs. Mavis

Smith, the present supervisor, and Mrs. Laura Keaton, R.N. Their daily encouragement strengthens me. The friendship of the volunteers who work with Mrs. Alderman, Mrs. Dorcas Peterson, Mrs. B. C. Hyatt, and Mrs. Betty Moore, helps to give meaning to my life.

I pray God's blessings on all who read this book and pray that it will cause other people to take notice of those in the nursing homes around them. Then others whose lives are wrecked and in need of rehabilitation, as mine was, will learn that God is good and that life can have meaning.

Sincerely,

DALE MIDDLEBROOKS

Preface

"Heart attacks," states *World Book Encyclopedia,* "are the greatest single cause of death in the United States. Every day they kill about 1,600 persons and leave thousands of others crippled to some extent for the rest of their lives."

I have heard the statement "The *worst* thing about a heart attack is the fact that it sometimes does *not* kill."

That is a strong statement, one that many people would be horrified to hear. I was not horrified to hear it. As one of the "thousands of others crippled to some extent for the rest of their lives," I understand what the person meant.

For three almost unendurable years I often felt the same way. I had lived an active life. Then my life pattern changed to one of such limited activity that the frustration was almost more than I could bear.

One day when it seemed I could not live another minute with my limitations, but knowing I had to do so, I asked my doctor, "Will you tell me just one worthwhile work I can be active enough to do?" For a moment he looked back toward a sort of plaque that showed the heart and its intricate workings. He had been using it to explain to me the nature of my particular problem. Then he looked directly into my eyes and patiently answered, "Remember your faith in God."

To remember and return to the grass roots of one's faith in God does not cause the physical part of heart disease to go away. It does, however, bring about a dramatic cure for the frustrations that may cause us to look down the days of our remaining years with a sickening sense of dread.

This "cure" that God can and will perform in the life of a physically handicapped person is not a meaningless escape from reality. It's also not a hobby. When given the chance to work his will in a life, God leads the person of limited strength into the kind of life that is rewarding to both self and others.

God has a new destiny for every person whose former way of life has been swept away by illness or accident. When this person hears and responds to God's call to work, in what may be a hitherto unthought-of "field," there is no longer the feeling that "the worst thing about a heart attack is that it sometimes does not kill."

Only God himself can know what he has in mind for you. A return, however, to the "Author and Finisher of your faith" and to a humbler and closer walk with him will bring you and your new destiny together. When at first you begin to recognize just where it is he's leading you, it may be that you'll feel as I did. I flatly stated, "nobody in his right mind would voluntarily go within a mile of such a place!"

And I did not go! That is, until God performed a miracle and enabled me to see the work through his eyes and to love it with a love which only he could have given me the capacity for.

The people I work with have responded so well to my suggestions that they "sing the Lord's song in their own strange lands" that they in turn have found new destinies. Many of them are dying, but their aim in life is no longer simply waiting for death. They are busy.

This book is my effort to tell their story. Their rare brand of courage may inspire hope in others who are victims of heart disease, accidents, nervous breakdowns, and the devastations of age. They have learned to think of themselves as something other than a vast and barren wasteland of humanity waiting to die. They have regained their dignity as human beings.

It is also, of course, the story of my own heart disease and new destiny. It is shared in the fervent hope that others who may feel as useless as I did will discover the same heartening truth which changed my life—that until our last breath is drawn, God has a worthwhile work for us *all* to do.

To the Reader

Nursing homes compose a new and almost untouched frontier in this era of time.

New ones are under construction, and present ones are being enlarged. Yet they grow more crowded by the day.

The "spaces" in them are occupied by *people,* not things. Not merely bodies called "residents." They are whole human beings.

These people are older and in poorer health than most of us.

But their emotions are as keenly sensitive as yours or mine. They love deeply. They also experience times of anger and frustration.

At times they smile and say, "There is a better day up ahead." Other times a plaintive voice laments, "I'm just not getting anywhere."

Some are loved and cherished by *many* friends and relatives who visit them daily. Others also have *many* relatives—somewhere; but they cannot remember when last they saw one of them.

Some of them pray in faith, believing that "All things work together for good to them that love God, to them who are the called according to his purpose."

Still others do not pray. They are outside God's fold and desperately need someone to lead them in.

I have a deep respect for our "caring society," especially the Christian segment of it. I am convinced that if our people get a glimpse of this hitherto-untouched frontier, a vast change for the better will come about.

The purpose of this book is to open the doors of nursing homes across our land and enable a caring society to envision the mission opportunity that beckons there.

Walking across the pages of the book are men and women who knew not how to sing the Lord's song in their own strange lands. Strange lands? Heartbreakingly so. Imagine the devastation in a human life when cataclysmic forces beyond his control converge upon him, sometimes with lightning swiftness, and sweep him into a strange and new life pattern. Health is gone. So is the home he loved for a lifetime.

Those you will meet in this book learned to sing the Lord's song in their own particular strange lands. They have ceased their backward looks toward homes to which they can never return. They comfort one another and lighten their own hearts with the knowledge that there really *is* a better day up ahead.

Getting them to really sing the Lord's song rather than hanging their hearts and talents on the walls of memory and weeping their days away did not come about easily or overnight.

Along with the seven years of my own work with them has gone the strengthening influence of cooperative staff members in the nursing home. Dr. J. W. Branch, Sr., owner of the home, is in total sympathy with the work that's done and often says so. My every effort is undergirded by Mrs. Dorcas Kersh Peterson and Mrs. Betty Whitlow Moore, who are *unfailingly* there. They play the piano, sing, and offer each resident their loving God-bless-you handshake.

The folks in Heritage Manor Nursing Home have a witness to bear and a story to tell. This book is my effort to tell it for them. It's their earnest prayer and mine that this story will act as seeds planted in hearts to bear rich fruit in other nursing homes.

Contents

1
Lord, Are You Telling Me Something?

"It's no use speaking to *her*. She doesn't even know she's in the world!"

The words startled me. I'd been moving toward a bed in a semidarkened room, meaning to speak to the one lying there, unaware that anyone else was nearby.

"I'm sorry," the nurse's aide continued, "but that lady's in a coma; and there's nothing you can do for her."

Stopping short, I looked briefly toward the still form, then left the room and returned home to put some supper together.

But something was wrong. The meal just would not come along, despite my ability to get one together with my eyes closed. The deathlike silence of the room that I'd just left pounded against my eardrums until I had no choice but to kneel down and pray.

"Lord," I fervently asked, "are you *telling* me something?"

His answer was as clear as if I'd heard his voice audibly. "Go back. Speak to that woman."

As soon as I could turn things off in the kitchen, I went back. Without pausing to even speak to those I met along the way, I went into the room I'd left such a short while ago.

What I did then was more difficult than returning to the room had been. But it was something I had to do. I walked to the lady's side, put my hand on her shoulder, and said, "God bless you."

Every night I'd pray for the silent and still person whose shoulder I'd touched that day. I often wondered what the folks who saw me doing that from day to day were thinking about me. It bothered me a little. But then I'd always encourage myself by remembering that God was the one to whom I must answer.

And I knew he meant me to go on with that seemingly futile task.

It got no easier, only harder. Sometimes it would seem that to touch her shoulder one more time was just more than I could do. But I'd do it.

One day, weeks later, I started toward her bed, fearing it would be that day I'd fail to touch her and to speak to her. I made it to her door, stopped, looked at her for a while, then turned to leave.

But I couldn't do it. I didn't know why, but I knew I had to walk on over and put my hand on her shoulder and say, "God bless you."

I did so hurriedly, then turned to leave. As I was turning, my heart seemed to stop its beating. The words, spoken haltingly, "God . . . bless . . . you . . . too," came to my ears.

"Oh!" I wept, clutching her hand. "You *heard* me!"

"Yes," came her answer.

I told her then what I'd been doing and for how long and that I knew God meant I should. Over and over she said, "Thank you for coming. Thank you for saying, 'God bless you' to me every day. Thank you for praying for me every night."

"I know I'm going to hell," the man said; "and when I get there, I'll have a lot of company. Now you get out of my room!"

"All right!" I answered. "But don't be expecting to see *me* in hell. I have other plans." I went from his room almost as angry as he. But I returned almost immediately. With my Bible in my hand I asked earnestly, "Sir, would you please let me read some of the Psalms to you?"

For a while he made no answer. Praying hard for strength and help, I began reading through many comforting chapters.

Then I heard him weeping softly and gently asking, "Will you forgive me?"

"Oh, yes, sir!" I answered, "if you'll promise me just one thing."

"What's that?"

"Please, sir, change your mind about going to hell. Jesus died to save you. Will you trust him?"

The soft weeping continued, but a smile of gentle and peaceful warmth spread over his face as he answered, "Yes, I'll be a Christian. Thank you for coming back!"

"I'm leaving this wheelchair at the door when I get to heaven," said a man, just over forty years old, who'd been disabled in an accident.

Before his accident, however, he'd not known Jesus as Savior. He found him in a nursing home.

One of my life's chief joys is the fact that I helped him and others to find Jesus as Lord and Savior. I also rejoice in the knowledge that I'm living in the very eye of the will of God.

It hasn't always been so. There was a time, just after I turned fifty, when I refused to see his will. I continued, unmindful of many clear indications as to the exact work God was calling me to do.

It is dangerous to tamper with the will of God. And neglecting to think of the highly unusual events in one's life as God's directing is to show God's will less respect than it deserves.

A neighbor up the street from where I live in Hope, Arkansas, took me along one day when she went to visit her mother in a local nursing home. Without even questioning whether my reaction to the encounter was God's attempt to tell me something, I thought only of getting away. That's what I did, vowing never again to go within a mile of such a place. I am not proud to admit it; but while I was there I did not shake hands with, speak to, or even smile at one lonely person.

It's an established medical fact that quiet, peaceful mental attitudes and good physical health go together. And it's an indisputable spiritual fact that apart from the assurance of being within the framework of God's will, there can be no peace of mind. For that reason I've wondered a thousand times if my husband Edwin and I might have been spared the turbulent upheaval that nearly wrecked my life had I attached some significance to the storm that arose in me during the visit to that nursing home. In retrospect, I'm unable to understand just how I could have dismissed the event from my mind, as I'd always felt that one should be careful to find the specific task God had planned for him. Down the centuries God had sometimes employed what seemed strange methods of communicating his will. How strange Elisha's instructions that he be provided with "a little cake" must have sounded to the widow who was preparing her last morsel of food, expecting that she and her son should then starve.

My utter revulsion to the people in the nursing home was out of character with me. All my life elderly folks have been very special to me. Everywhere I've ever lived, I've regularly visited and ministered to them, especially those who were bedridden. So why did I react as I did on that occasion? If I'd prayed that question through then, this might have been a far different story. Surely it would have been a better witness to the faith in God I professed to have at the time. But I did not pray. I ran.

Not long afterward Edwin began asking rather often, "Why are you breathing so hard?" At first I merely shrugged the question off. Then one night he persisted, and I got annoyed. After denying that I was breathing hard, I went into another room and went to sleep. A few hours later, though, he was asking urgently, "Darling, what's the matter? Are you hurting anywhere?" I nodded yes.

The next thing I clearly recall out of the kaleidoscopic maze of events that followed was my wondering why Dr. Browning was mad at me. I was in Highland Hospital in Shreveport, Louisiana. He was standing at my door with an expression so serious that it seemed he must either be impatient with me (which he never was) or very bothered about something. "You've had a coronary thrombosis," he said, "and I'm ordering changes in your way of living." He was and is my friend as well as my doctor. This accounted for his serious expression.

That was May 1966. From then until May 1969 my life was a continuous nightmare. I had been just about as active as a person could be. With our two daughters grown (Linda had finished college and married; Libby was still in college), I was at last free to do more of the things I liked. My time was spent designing and making our clothes, digging the yard and cutting the grass, entertaining a church or club group, driving to Huntsville, Alabama, to visit our three-year-old granddaughter Sharon

Horn, or going with Edwin on a weekend trip into the nearby Ozark mountains. It was a good life.

Dr. Browning's words "I am ordering some changes in your way of living" did not upset me. They just didn't register. How was I to comprehend the whole meaning? The terrible pain I'd had before going to the hospital seemed almost to have been a dream—that is, until a day or so after I returned home.

The temperature had climbed to a hot and dry one hundred degrees, and the grass I'd tended with so much pride was wilting. I went outside and sat under a tree while holding the water hose and sprinkling the grass, moving on from time to time to other spots in the yard. In a very short while, however, I realized with a jolt that I was not enjoying the job as I'd expected to. I went inside, meaning to rest awhile.

As soon as I reached the air-conditioned house my chest began hurting, and I was nauseated. When the pain got worse Dr. Lowell Harris, my local doctor at the time, was called in. On his first trip to see me, the magnitude of the changes that my life was to undergo began to penetrate my thoughts and make me uneasy. He explained that my heart could not adjust to drastic temperature changes as rapidly as in the past and that I'd have to be careful. I was not ready yet to be careful or even convinced that I'd have to be. It required more pain and some trips to the hospital to convince me, and at that point my real crisis began.

The extent of my curtailed activity was really impressed upon me some time later when I called the doctor and asked if I could take a walk. "Yes," he answered, "walk slowly in your backyard." I was so disappointed at first that I didn't even bother to walk at all. Then I went on and did as he said and got sick again. That alarmed me. The very idea of being as inactive as it appeared I'd have to be was too much, and I rebelled with every breath I drew. Of course, that made my recovery even slower.

Time passed, but my life pattern became no easier to live with. Instead it became almost unbearably frustrating, and I got more and more depressed. Dr. Harris began eventually to urge that I again use my talent for teaching the Bible, but I wasn't interested. It was months before I'd understand why this hith-erto-fascinating task no longer appealed to me. I was thinking only in terms of classes taught at church. I learned, though, that there were other places where Bible lessons would be appre-ciated. Near desperation drove me to challenge Dr. Harris one day to tell me just one worthwhile work I could be active enough to do. He patiently answered, "Remember your faith in God."

His answer stunned me.

Slowly and without heart, I returned home feeling more adrift and alone than I'd ever felt in my life. I sat for hours thinking, or trying to think. Faith in God? Did I have faith in God? My question startled me, but strangely enough I felt better for having asked it. I honestly did not know the answer, but an indefinable something began to take shape in my thoughts that afternoon. Perhaps it was the stirring of a dormant faith. *What,* I wondered, *should be a test whereby I could know whether I remembered my faith? Faith without works is dead,* I reasoned. *What works could I do?*

I could write get-well cards. Letters I'd written through the years had seemed to help people. The hundreds I'd received since my illness encouraged me, and some of those had been written by people who were far worse off than I. I had improved enough to drive my car. Some of the folks who had faithfully prayed for me were shut-ins and could not drive or even go out. A visit from me might do a little toward brightening those folks' dreary hours.

I called the chairman of the nominating committee for the women's work in our church and asked to serve on the Mission Action Group. My contribution could be writing get-well cards and making some visits to shut-ins. I shall never forget how encouraged I felt when Mrs. Henry Haynes answered, "We have already put your name down as a worker in that group."

That short phone call put me within a heartbeat of a whole new destiny, as deeply meaningful and rewarding as a person could long for. The destiny whose threshold I approached was to draw more people into its framework than anyone, other than God, could begin to count.

My very first glimpse into it, however, proved to be a near disaster.

I was assigned the task of going to Branch Manor Nursing Home and getting the names and birthdays of new residents and the names of those who had died.

I was horrified! *Nobody* in his right mind would *voluntarily* go near such a place! I said as much and naturally was not asked to go again.

2
The Lord's Song in a Strange Land

Weeks turned into months. Each one made me a bit more empty and restless than the other. I helped with all the good works the Mission Action Group did and was heartily in favor of every one. But my boredom at helping with them very nearly sickened me. I longed to work with people on a person-to-person basis and was fully convinced that what I was doing was not God's will for my life.

I enjoyed some of the work I did—letter writing and visits to the sick—but something was missing. I longed for a *continuing* work. Still, I had no desire to teach a class at church.

Then something wonderful happened as quietly on my part as a snowflake falling in the night.

At the group meeting of the Mission Action Committee in May 1969 I was my usual bored self. Then the chairman announced, "We need a Bible teacher for Heritage Manor Nursing—" "I'll do that!" I hurriedly said before the announcement was even finished, as though I feared someone else would get that wondrous task before I could speak!

I don't imagine those women had ever been more startled in their lives. They were bound to have wondered just what had happened to me, remembering the static I'd given them when I was asked to go to a nursing home for only a few minutes.

But there was no need for *me* to question what had happened.

I knew God had brought about a miracle. At the moment I said the words a benedictory peace settled about me, the first actual rest I'd known since Dr. Browning had interpreted the strange-looking markings called *tracings* on the electrocardiogram.

No longer were those in nursing homes just bodies waiting

to die. They were ill and lonely folks who could and would work creatively for God if someone would teach them to do so.

They were people who, needing love, needed even more to give love—to God, to their doctors and nurses, who like to be appreciated, and to their children, whose hearts are broken because they cannot keep their father or mother with them and care for their needs. They also needed to know that they were to love and serve one another and that in so doing they would be serving God and regaining their dignity as human beings.

Hurriedly, I went out to meet them. The supervisor, Mrs. Pauline Frazier, was a fellow church member whom I'd not met. All residents were polite and cool, except for one who wanted to know if I was married and quickly lost interest upon learning I was.

Wheelchairs. Blind folks. A "vegetable." Outright suspicion of me—one called me a Communist. Eyes staring into nowhere. A dying woman, concerned as to whether she would go to heaven or hell, but telling me quite frankly she thought hell's claim on her soul might have the upper edge.

Conservatively speaking, I had a challenge.

When the time came to prepare to teach, some disturbing questions came to my mind. What could I prepare that would be meaningful and have a practical application to those who could neither walk nor see? To a woman who didn't even know she was in the world? To another who was dying and unsure of her soul's salvation?

Never in all the years I'd taught the Bible had I prayed more honestly for God's leadership than on that occasion. And never was an answer clearer or a way made more plain than it was then. After praying I reached these conclusions. God has never retired anyone. He has a unique task at which each person is to be busy until he draws his dying breath. The man or woman in a wheelchair can go into the rooms of the bedfast and cheerfully pass the time of day for a while. The blind person can pray for many people who might not be taking the time to pray for themselves. Bedfast people can smile at nurses and doctors. None of us can measure the inspiration we get by seeing a cheerful smile from a suffering person. The man or woman who is dying is as obligated before God to be a Christian witness as is the one who still has good health.

With these things in mind I prepared the first lesson they were to hear from the Bible since going to a nursing home to live. I used the first four verses of Psalm 137, an account of God's people hanging their harps in the willow trees and weeping, refusing to sing the Lord's song in their strange land of captivity.

I urged *them* to sing the Lord's song in their own particular strange lands of pain, of loneliness, and of the heartbreak of leaving their homes, knowing they would never again see them. Leaving home under such conditions is a devastating experience. I told them that if they would do their very best, despite their heartaches, they would in a manner of speaking be "singing the Lord's song." I continued, using the parable of the talents as recorded in Matthew 25 to stress my point, "If you do whatever you can do, *right here where you are,* Heritage Manor Nursing Home will become a place for you to call your home. It will be the kind of place where every one of you can regain your dignity and grasp the knowledge that you are still a part of humanity. The person outside God's fold will find Jesus Christ as Savior, and not one of you will be without a friend."

The moment I stood up to begin this first lesson Mr. Crews demanded, "*Who* sent *you* out here?" "God," I answered, smiling, and got on with what I had prepared to say. Apparently he liked my answer—he never missed a class except at times when he was in the hospital. I believe they were pleased by the fact that I treated them with respect, as men and women, not as babies needing to be coddled. Their attitude toward my teaching was as appreciative as I could have hoped for. We only had ten or twelve present the first week, but those few worked so faithfully that every resident except the bedfast and one other attended from then on.

That initial lesson, on May 28, 1969, took them by surprise. But the manner in which they met the challenge would have warmed any teacher's heart.

3
My Ten-talented Friends

It was soon apparent that I had some ten-talented friends at Heritage Manor. One of these was Dale Middlebrooks. His response was the first indication I had that my teaching was being taken seriously. He gripped my hand after a teaching session one day, looked me level in the eye, and said a simple "Thank you." The expression on his face said, "I believe you."

Soon after my lessons began, he started offering his help to staff members and residents alike. After about two years I became convinced that I should ask permission for him to attend Sunday School and church with Edwin and me if he wanted to. (His religious background was the same as ours, Southern Baptist. Had it been otherwise, I'd have told his answer to the pastor of the church of his choice. The work I do is financially supported by First Baptist Church, mainly by the Woman's Missionary Union [WMU], and by Dr. J. W. Branch, Sr., a Presbyterian and owner of the home. But in no way do I ever try to influence patients toward a denominational stance—I just teach the Bible.)

When I asked Mrs. Revis' permission to invite him to attend church with us, she readily answered, "Of course! That would be a good thing to do." I then asked him if he'd be interested. There was humble pathos in his answer: "I surely would like to go if you are sure you and Mr. Alderman wouldn't mind my going with you." My heart still breaks when I remember the way he looked as he spoke.

As the three of us approached the entrance to the educational building on that first Sunday morning, I was frankly scared, wondering how things would go. He was well dressed, and my church is as friendly as one could possibly be; still, I was uneasy. But I needn't have been. The moment we got inside Rose Luck, my best friend, exclaimed, "Dale Middlebrooks!" as she threw her arms around him. They had attended college together. In opening assembly Frank King, superintendent, said, "Well! I'm glad to see a college buddy of mine, Dale Middlebrooks," as he walked up to shake his hand in welcome.

A few weeks later I asked Mr. Middlebrooks if he had thought about becoming a Christian. He is keenly intelligent and deeply sensitive, and I was of the opinion that he couldn't possibly have listened to the sermons Brother Trussell preached without having done some thinking on the matter.

His ready reply was, "Yes, Mrs. Alderman, I have; and I would like to talk to Brother Trussell." That is the kind of request I particularly like to pass on to my pastor and the kind he likes most to get. He went immediately. Minutes after his visit Mr. Middlebrooks called to tell me quite happily, "I am now a Christian and am going to unite with your church and be baptized Sunday."

His had been a tragic life, fraught with storms that would have devastated a lesser person. According to him and his sister, Cathryn Tedder, who stood by him through a series of illnesses, his coming to Heritage Manor was a last desperate hope for a place to live that would meet his medical needs. The doctor had in fact frankly told them both there was next to no hope that his health would ever improve.

But when, despite his loneliness and poor health, he began ministering to those whose paths were even darker than his own, there shone across his horizon the light of renewed hope. He was destined to become an integral part of a volunteer team of workers I would organize later. He works with the zeal of a missionary, doing more in a day to cheer the lonely than most of us do in a lifetime. Radio station KXAR here in Hope once honored him with a fitting tribute and dedicated to him the song "Brighten the Corner Where You Are." He reads the Scriptures and leads in prayer at each Bible class. He ministers during the week to residents who are in sorrow or trouble of any kind. He calls me at times when it is necessary for me to visit residents.

In response to my challenge that the patients rediscover the joy in life that work could afford, Mrs. Daisy Phillips, a lovely black amputee, began working on a quilt, taking special pains to match pieces and create something beautiful.

They took my suggestion that they manifest their love toward God by doing good for one another. On the day Mrs. Lillie Fowler's only son died, her room was filled with sympathetic friends, some coming by wheelchair, others with the aid of walkers.

Mrs. Ethel Taylor, her voice trembling and weak, said to me one day after class, "I am going to read the Bible to that blind lady." She faithfully did so for as long as she could be understood at all. My life was deeply enriched by that fine little lady's example.

Mrs. Mittie Kelton puts fresh clothes on a partially helpless lady several times a day.

Mrs. Bessie Mohon, more than ninety years old and able to get about only with a walker, goes regularly into the rooms of those who cannot be up and visit with them. She interrupts many a soap opera, but nobody within her range could possibly feel neglected. She is a woman of such indomitable strength that she inspires us volunteers to keep on working even when we get tired.

Mr. Cleveland Brewer cheerfully entered into the spirit of the work that was going on by making daily wheelchair visits up and down the halls.

Mr. Osborne Chambers is constantly in severe pain but is so cheerful and good natured that it's an inspiration to me to be around him.

Mr. Thomas O'Brien, though unable to hear even the faintest sound, faithfully attends every class and encourages us on every hand. His exceptional reading ability along with his eagerness to be of help to us proved a great blessing on one occasion. While wondering whom I might get to read the Bible on Wednesday mornings while Mr. Middlebrooks was in the hospital, there came to my mind the thought that Mr. O'Brien might like to do it. Nurse Thelma Stone and I mentioned this to him and were deeply touched by the smile that spread over his lonely face. He readily agreed to help us and did so for several weeks. Residents, staff members, and volunteers will long remember the thrill we got from witnessing his joy. We fervently wished he might have heard the rousing "Amen" he got after each of his readings.

I loved Mrs. Bessie Vines even before she became a part of our Heritage Manor family. She is the only one I knew prior to beginning my work at the nursing home. Until the death of Mr. Vines, they lived across the highway from our farm. At any time the electric current went off in the complex housing our fifty thousand laying hens, she would call Edwin and report the trouble. Her voice on the telephone was an almost daily occurrence, so it came as no surprise that she could always find someone to do a favor for when she went to live at the nursing home.

Getting adjusted to her strange surroundings was rough on her, though. One day she wept bitterly and said, "Oh! I am so homesick I can't bear it." But the next time I saw her she was dressed beautifully and was smiling as she mingled with other residents. When I commented on this she observed, "This is now my home, and I'm going to make the best of it."

Mrs. Vesta Williams was another who had seen an unusual number of tragedies in her life. These took their toll and she lost her health, though she was not of an age to have been disabled. There came a day when, due to a flu epidemic, we volunteers could not go to the nursing home. She was not physically up to playing the piano for their Wednesday service, but she did and did it well. Afterward she said to me, "I'll never do that again." But she did. It took courage, but courage is something I see a lot of as I go from room to room visiting the folks at Heritage Manor.

4
Courage and a New Destiny

An example of this courage has been evidenced in the husbands and wives of the nursing-home residents. They live in strange lands of aloneness, too deep to be fathomed by anyone except God himself. Some walk out and get a divorce. This must undoubtedly be the crowning heartbreak to one whose body has been broken in an accident, but I've seen it happen. There have been others, though, who stood by, loving in times of trouble as they did in happier days.

One of these was Mrs. Maxine Hamilton, whose husband Robert was so disabled by an accident that he could not even feed himself. I shall never forget the shock I felt when first I met him. I was visiting in the rooms when I saw a fairly young man— still in his forties. Thoughtlessly I asked, "Why are *you* in a nursing home?" As I asked the question, though, I realized he'd been in a crippling accident and apologized for my abruptness. After we'd talked for a while he told me he wanted me to become acquainted with his wife and gave me her telephone number.

As soon as I returned home I called her. Then at her request I went to see her. I had expected to find a very troubled person and was partially prepared for that. But her despair went beyond what I'd counted on—her husband was not a Christian, and the fact was distressing her almost beyond endurance.

We had prayer for him then and agreed to pray for him daily.

She visited him every day and communicated her love to him in all the ways one could express love. After a while he began attending our Bible classes, and she was always by his side. There came the day when he spoke out and said, "I have accepted Jesus as my Savior." There was never a happier woman than

Maxine was that day; and if ever one deserved to feel good, she did. I believe it was her love and faithfulness to him, while living in her own heartbreaking loneliness, that paved the way for him to believe in God.

I try to help those whom I teach to grasp the idea that each of them does indeed have a unique role in God's creative work.

Believing that the sick and elderly who rightly use their opportunities to pray can help bring about marvelous things, I gave them definite prayer assignments. One was that they pray daily for the lost among them to find the Lord.

One day I saw their faces transformed as they heard one for whom they had been praying interrupt the lesson to say he had taken Jesus as his Savior.

Soon after that heartening experience, they began praying for a little girl, one very dear to me. Her name is Sharon. She had just turned six, a kindergarten graduate, when, during her summer vacation, she began going with me to visit at the nursing home. She would follow along after me, shaking the people's hands and saying, "God bless you," just as she saw me do.

After one of the Bible lessons she seemed disturbed and asked, "Grandmother, am I going to heaven?"

"Yes," I answered, "if you take Jesus as your Savior."

When the folks whom she had been visiting with me heard about this, they began praying for her daily. A few months after her eighth birthday, we shared the joy of learning she had become a Christian.

Yes, much of my task as a teacher has been the sheer joy of sharing with a group of people some of God's answers to definite prayer assignments.

Another joy my new destiny affords is the hope that it helps concerning race relations. I had not known that the patients were integrated when I volunteered to teach them.

I had grown up believing integration was not even a nice word. In the structured society I had known, to address a black person as "Mr." or "Mrs." was unheard of. And for a white woman to shake hands with a black man would have been akin to indecency, in the eyes of my parents. But, after some earnest praying, this problem dissolved into nothingness. I believe it is right, in the sight of God, to shake hands with everyone. That is what I did and soon realized that I loved both races equally.

A few months after I began teaching, a black man, with tears streaming down his face, said, "Teacher, I didn't give my heart to the Lord until I saw that you loved my people."

When Mr. Ambrose Harris, an elderly black man who had been making a serious study of "white teacher" (frankly believing I was a phony), realized I loved those of his race, he asked me which northern state I had come from. My reply, "I grew up in south Mississippi," was a great big joke to him, which he steadfastly refused to believe until four months later when he learned I had visited a relative there. I have a warm spot in my heart for my native state and was glad when Mr. Harris finally admitted to feeling friendly toward it too.

This work is for me a new destiny, encouraging me to hope that I am a part of God's creative plan. But it is no escape from the reality of heart disease and its limitations. Six months after beginning it, another heart attack resulted in my being able to tolerate even fewer heartbeats a minute. Severe pain sometimes plunges me into the depths of despair.

At such times I try to recall words of C. S. Lewis to the effect that when a human no longer desiring, but still intending, to do God's will looks around a universe from which every trace of God seems to have vanished and asks why he has been forsaken, yet still obeys, Satan's cause is in danger.

However, those words had an almost empty ring to them after my second heart attack. Satan's cause seemed to have gained momentum against what I was trying to do at Heritage Manor. For weeks the folks had no Bible lessons; and I saw no hope that there would be any for some time, as I was scheduled to go into a Little Rock hospital for treatment.

But my pastor sensed my distress over their having no Bible lessons and volunteered to teach them for me. It was three months before I could return to the work, and I'm sure he was burdened with the work load. But not once did he mention it.

Dr. Ben Price, my cardiologist, promised that I'd eventually feel better. But even at the time I returned to my work at Heritage, I couldn't see much evidence that I would do so. I'd become exhausted so easily that it depressed me. In order then for the work to continue, it was necessary to get a whole team of full-time volunteers to assist me. It was obvious to me that I could no longer function as independently as I had been doing.

5
Life Could Still Have Meaning

The volunteer needed most at the time was a substitute teacher, someone I could count on to be ready at a moment's notice to teach when I could not go. With my particular health handicap there are times when I have no chance to plan ahead. This would have been a problem situation except for the attitude toward the work that Gerald W. Trussell, my pastor, had.

While teaching the patients during the three months of my illness, he had learned to know and love them in that very special way with which only pastors seem to be acquainted. They, in the meantime, had come to feel equally as close to him. So it should have come as no surprise on the day he said to me, "Now, Rosalie, I don't want you worrying about who might help you at the nursing home because I want to go when you can't." That was more than six years ago. He still goes when I cannot and does so as cheerfully now as he did then.

My honest opinion is that, without his eager interest in this mission, it never could have gotten off the ground. With humility I can say that my substitute teacher is none other than my pastor. This isn't to suggest that he neglects our church in order to help at Heritage. He pastors a large flock and is never far away when one of us is in any kind of trouble. When in the hospital, whether here or further away, we can count on him to be by our sides as soon as he can get there.

He preaches, too, with all the fervor and eloquence of a modern-day apostle Paul. I doubt that any pastor on earth is busier than he, which makes me feel all the more humble as I think of his attitude toward the work at Heritage Manor.

Mrs. Mae Bell Revis, who took Mrs. Pauline Frazier's place as supervisor when the latter resigned, was at Heritage Manor when I returned from Little Rock. I recall that the warm friendliness of her greeting as we were introduced cheered me and that her promise, "I'm going to see that a piano is brought here to help with your work," made no impression on me. I didn't expect anything to come of it, but that was only because I did not know Mrs. Revis. She told her church—Garrett Memorial Baptist—about the need, and they provided one right away. As the weeks went by, it became apparent that she was, in every sense of the word, a volunteer worker in all I was trying to do at the nursing home.

So it was only natural that I should invite her to be a part of the work, in name as well as in deed. She eagerly responded to my invitation to be on the list of volunteers; and if anyone ever lived up to a promise, she did. Without the supervisor's sympathy and cooperation, no one could hope to do an effective work with the residents of a nursing home. I have been fortunate in that the three supervisors who have been at Heritage Manor during my seven years of work have all been kind, courteous, and wholly cooperative with all my efforts.

I recall an instance when my answer to a question of Mrs. Revis' caused her to weep. Upon my arrival one Wednesday morning soon after she became supervisor, she asked me, "Why do you dress up just to come out here?" "Because," I replied, "I respect these folks, and if I dress in my best clothes to teach them, they'll know they're important to me." She and I worked closely together five years, and a friendship grew between us that will endure for a long time, for as long as we live.

Soon after the piano was donated, Mrs. B. C. Hyatt volunteered to be our pianist. She is a gracious lady and one of the best musicians in Arkansas. She served as our pianist for nearly six years, until she resigned to become organist for the First Presbyterian Church. She still comes to us when our regular pianist cannot get there.

When Mrs. Hyatt came I began leading the folks in the singing of hymns; but the effort proved to be a bit more than I could physically handle. I was too exhausted to teach afterward. This started me looking and praying for a full-time song leader to assist me. As it turned out, my search didn't last long. Mrs. Billie Russell, who sings in our church choir on Sunday mornings, sat beside me in church on the Sunday night following my decision to find a song leader. Listening to her that night, I knew my search was over, provided she was free on Wednesday mornings. She was, and she agreed so graciously to my request that I knew she was actually looking forward to working with us.

Billie, a very talented and friendly young lady, soon won the hearts of all the residents—especially Mr. Harris, who was by then rejoicing in his wonderful discovery that white folks could love him. He affectionately referred to Billie as "that singing woman."

I met Mrs. Rose Luck at a WMU meeting at First Baptist Church just two days after we moved to Hope. The friendship that instantly grew between us is still something very special. She shared flowering shrubs (we'd moved into a new home), bulbs, and trees with me. When, a year later, I became seriously ill, she proved to be the proverbial "friend in deed." On one particularly bad day I lay in my hospital room thinking about her and wishing I could go to her. Her husband had died three days previously, and I could not even call her on the telephone. I shall never forget that, as I lay there grieving for her, she came in to see about me.

She had put her own grief aside in her concern for me. I was to go by ambulance two days later to a Dallas hospital where I would have an angiogram and possible heart surgery.

Rose was chairman of the Mission Action Group two years later when I volunteered to teach the Bible and minister to the residents at Heritage Manor. She was also the one to whom I'd said a few months earlier, "Don't *ever* ask me to go near a nursing home again because I never mean to go anywhere close to one!"

When I began thinking in terms of who to ask to assist me in visiting the folks, it was natural that Rose should be my choice. I asked her to help and she readily consented, as I knew she would. She is still "one of us" and is faithful to visit those who are hospitalized or in sorrow. She can be counted on to send cards to those having birthdays, to help us financially when such a need arises, and above all else to stand by us with her moral support.

Another friend, Mrs. Marie Gunter, volunteered to be a visitor soon after Rose joined our team. She is also a faithful helper whom we can always depend on. A more compassionate person than she could not be found, and we are fortunate to have her help. She is now quite busy as chairman of the Mission Action Group but still takes the time to visit regularly at the nursing home.

After a few months Billie resigned as song leader to become a teacher in a Hope school. On one of the Wednesdays that we were without a leader, Mrs. Dorcas Peterson was invited to help us. I knew Dorcas only casually at the time and was somewhat reluctant to ask her to help us. But Dorcas came. She was shy, sweet, and very pretty. And she sang like an angel. Sensing her sweet attitude toward the folks, I lost no time in asking her to work with us full-time. She not only accepted but told me awhile later that she had been praying for God to lead her into just such a work.

And what a work she does! She too is one of the very best of musicians, being not only an able song leader but an accomplished pianist, organist, and soloist as well. Residents, staff members, volunteers, and guests thrill to her solos each week. She has been my co-worker and my right hand in the work for five years and is so dedicated that she never misses a service except when ill or on vacation.

The next person we invited to serve with us was Dale Middlebrooks, a resident. It's at this point that I so fervently wish for more ability to use words. Only then could I describe the joy which that fine gentleman brings to his fellow residents, to his church, and especially to all of us volunteers. We depend on his help all through the week and particularly on Wednesday mornings.

I first heard him read the Bible and speak on a morning when, due to a flu epidemic, the nursing home was quarantined; and we volunteers could not go for the services. With Mrs. Revis' cooperation, I arranged, by telephone, for the folks to hold their own service. Words cannot express the feelings I had when I answered the phone that morning and heard Mrs. Revis say, "Listen!" She placed the phone so I could hear the singing and Mr. Middlebrooks' remarks quite well.

Only God himself can know the thrill I received. It was a time to ponder again Dr. Lowell Harris' words to me, "Remember your faith in God."

After that thrilling experience, I asked Mr. Middlebrooks to serve on our volunteer team as Resident Chaplain. He hesitated briefly, feeling unworthy of the honor. He accepted the job, though, after I assured him that Brother Trussell and every member of the volunteer team were in agreement that he should do it.

When I'm tired and discouraged about the work I remember something Mr. Middlebrooks wrote to my daughter, Linda Horn, thanking her for a Bible she had sent him. He wrote, "When I came to Heritage Manor I was at my rope's end. I had given up hope. Then I began listening to your mother's Bible teaching and realized that my life could still have meaning."

The manner in which he works for God in his strange land of loneliness and illness is an inspiration to all of us who go regularly to the nursing home. We know that, because of the hours of hard work we put in, wrecked lives are being rehabilitated. And that's reason enough to rejoice, even at times when we don't feel so well.

Mr. Middlebrooks still attends Sunday School and church at First Baptist with Edwin and me. He is well thought of by the folks at church and deeply loved by the folks at Heritage Manor where he faithfully serves, though his health is very poor.

While Mrs. Betty Moore was WMU President, she found her way out to our Bible classes often, sometimes to fill in for the song leader or the pianist, sometimes to help in other ways. As time passed and I sensed her growing love for the folks, I invited her to join our team. Her gracious reply was "How nice of you to ask me!" She is a beautiful woman who knows how to meet people well and to help them feel at ease. She is also a talented musician, and when Mrs. Hyatt began her work as organist at the Presbyterian church, she became our pianist.

Several months ago Betty began bringing her mother-in-law, Mrs. Jewel Moore, Sr., and Mrs. Ruth Porter along with her to our meetings. They contribute a great deal toward the good fellowship in the meetings. They have known some of the residents for many years. Their regular visits help the folks to believe that their former friends and neighbors still think of them.

It should have seemed that I now had enough help, but the work load grew by the day. Realizing that there might be some residents who would like to correspond with relatives and friends but who could no longer see to write or even in some cases hold a pen, I began writing letters for them. The letters were answered, in most cases sent to me to be read to the folks and to be answered in return.

Too, I tried to keep a record of each resident: birthday, church affiliation, relatives and their addresses. I wrote individual Christmas greetings to residents, to their families, and to staff members. It all finally became too much for me to handle.

Mrs. Maxine Hamilton came to my rescue by volunteering to be the secretary for the team. I protested, telling her it was too much for her to do that and minister to her husband at the nursing home as she did. The memory of what she said then moves me to tears. "Rosalie," she said, "I have been praying for God to open up a way for me to do something for you in appreciation for your leading my husband to the Lord." She serves faithfully and well, despite ill health and deep sorrow.

We were stunned when, early in 1974, Mrs. Revis, due to the illness of her husband, took early retirement. Residents and volunteers alike felt like orphans as we wondered if the next supervisor would be as good to us as she had been.

6
Fellow Helpers

I'm thankful to say that when Mrs. Mavis Smith became supervisor, she was keenly interested in our work and cooperated with us so wholeheartedly that I invited her to be a member of our team. Her gracious reply was "I would consider it an honor."

Mrs. Smith earned a warm place in our hearts by her faithful attendance upon Mrs. Bessie Mohon, who was dying. We had little hope that Mrs. Mohon would get better, but we hadn't counted on Mrs. Smith hovering over her throughout the night and literally spoon-feeding her back to life.

The time came when Mrs. Martha Folsom was too ill to attend Bible classes. None of us had any hope that she'd ever be better—none of us except Mrs. Smith, that is. Again she did not give up, and Mrs. Folsom is well enough to attend. She is a real joy to us in all the services we have.

In addition to the team of regular volunteers who work with me, there are many others whose help I could not easily do without. Edwin has eaten cold suppers at times when, due to the serious illness of a resident, I've been at the hospital or nursing home. There are times when it doesn't seem fitting that I should visit one of the men unless accompanied by my husband. He goes along on such occasions without a murmur, and this means a great deal to me. He gave me a brand-new electric typewriter that I could scarcely do without. It is used every week in preparing lesson helps. He helps to support the work financially and stands ready to help in more ways than I could name. He has taught for me several times.

The WMU, upon learning how exhausting it was for me to speak loud enough to be heard by the hard-of-hearing, installed a public address system for the home. This is an inestimable help. That same fine group of women, under the leadership of Mrs. Mabel Andrews, financed the repair of the system once when it broke down.

When the public address system was installed it occurred to me that the first words I should speak over it should be meaningful. I prayed earnestly about this before going out to test the system. When I stood I had no idea what I'd feel led to say, but immediately the following words came to my mind: "Jesus said, 'Go ye therefore, and teach all nations, baptizing them in the name of the Father, and of the Son, and of the Holy Ghost: Teaching them to observe all things whatsoever I have commanded you: and, lo, I am with you alway, even unto the end of the world.' "

I then prayed, asking God to so guide me that *my* teaching would help my hearers and myself to live closer to God.

Dr. J. W. Branch, Sr., who owns the home, is a staunch supporter of the work. I did not know him personally until I'd been teaching there for about four years. I had become so deeply involved in the work that it seemed wise to both Edwin and me for me to ask him to be my local physician. This was a difficult thing for me to do as Dr. Lowell Harris was and still is a friend to Edwin, to me, and to my whole family. I also felt that, except for his patient work with me, I might never have recovered enough to find my new destiny.

It was wise, though, to change to Dr. Branch because of his deep interest in the nursing home. During my first visit to him he voiced a real concern over the fact that the folks had never had a communion service. Right there he and I worked out a plan whereby one could be held right away.

He arranged for the Rev. Ralph Madison, pastor of First Presbyterian Church, to conduct the service. Mr. Comer Boyette, an elder, assisted him.

That communion service was deeply moving. Until then I'd never given a thought to the fact that those folks had not worshiped in that holy manner since coming to the home. Those who had found the Lord since coming to the home had *never* had the experience. Tears still dim my eyes when I remember the unashamed weeping of Mrs. Maxine Hamilton as she witnessed her husband partaking of the Lord's Supper for the first time. It was a doubly meaningful occasion in that it was also his *last* opportunity to worship in this manner.

I remember the expression on Mr. Hamilton's face and the deep hush that fell upon the whole congregation during the service. I'll never take part in another such service without thinking about that experience. Just about all denominations were represented, and it seemed to me that they all felt very close to God and to each other.

When Edwin bought me the typewriter, I sort of dragged my feet about starting to use it in my work. (I love to work with people and to write, but I'm not at all fond of any kind of mechanical work.) The day came, however, when my conscience demanded that I should decide on some way in which to put that marvelous piece of equipment to work for the Lord. I decided to write a bulletin to supplement our Bible study each week.

I went to the church office where Mrs. Hubert Thrash and Mrs. Francis Miller gave me some stencils and offered to help me in any way they could. I hurried home and began working up the bulletin and was quite elated as I anticipated the glad surprise I'd see on the residents' faces the next morning when I'd hand them the bulletins. Then I got my stencil to cut it, and right there my joy turned to that many ashes. I was so completely exhausted I could not go any further, and I was devastated.

I called Dorcas to lament the fact to her. She said, "I'll be right over." I thought to myself, *Now that's nice, but what has it got to do with getting the bulletin done?* She read it and said, "This is good. Where is your typewriter?" In an exhausted daze, I merely pointed and said, "Thataway!" She cut the stencil and asked, "Will you do the writing and let me do the rest?"

Just like that it happened. A new dimension to our nursing home ministry was born at that moment. Its reach was destined not only to include most of these United States but to span the oceans as well. It would be read by a lonely young soldier serving a tour of duty on the ghostly beaches of Okinawa. It would be read in other nursing homes in Hope as well as nursing homes in many other states. I would receive a phone call from a faraway state saying, "I read your personal message in the bulletin and made my mind up not to take my life." Another said, also by long-distance, "I read your article in the bulletin entitled 'Blessed Are the Peacemakers' and have decided not to get a divorce."

There were to be enough many-splendored responses to the messages in the bulletins to fill a book. But that was all in the future on the day when Dorcas stenciled that first one.

We only ran forty copies, thinking that would be more than enough. What we hadn't counted on was that staff members at Heritage Manor, Branch Manor, Branch General Hospital, relatives of residents, and scores of friends would request copies and that in a short while there would be a mailing list of nearly two hundred.

When postage became too much of a burden for me, the WMU, Edwin, Rose Luck, my sister Lillian Rogers, and many others shouldered the burden. First Baptist Church furnishes stencils, paper, and so forth.

The bulletin is a kind of miniature newsletter, containing items of news about residents. In a sense it's a link with the world outside, a means by which relatives stay in closer touch with their family members who are in the home.

One ministry of the bulletin which is sure to bear fruit in eternity is its telling our readers about "Our Mission." We joined the American Bible Society's Bible-a-Month Club in May 1973. The manner in which this came about is a deeply moving story within itself.

7
Expanding a Ministry

A new resident, Tommy Thomas, exclaimed at the end of the first Bible class he attended, "I had no idea there would be anything like *this* at a nursing home! I want to *contribute* something!" Only a few hours later, Mr. Thomas passed away. His words, however, lingered with me; and I began praying for God to reveal to me some kind of offering I could lead them to participate in. Being aware that the mere mention of giving to *anybody's* church would get me in trouble with those of some other denomination, I had to search for some worthy project unrelated to a church.

A gift of money came to me during the time I was praying for this worthy cause. Mrs. Lucy Davis' daughter, Mrs. Florence Coyner, was dying and had only weeks to live. She sent Mrs. Davis a generous gift of money to give to me, saying, "Tell her to use it in her work." Not knowing what to do with it, I kept it until God led us to "Our Mission." The money was then used as an enduring memorial to Mrs. Coyner, who had by that time passed away.

A few weeks after Mrs. Coyner sent the money, there came to me the wonderful realization that I might lead the folks to join the American Bible Society's Bible-a-Month Club. If only one Bible were sent each month, that would be a tremendous "gift that would never stop giving." With that in mind, I wrote the following words in the bulletin:

"Being your teacher gives rise to a feeling of motherliness toward you which causes me to feel (justifiably) guilty because I've not urged you to make financial contributions to a worthy cause. Don't stop reading yet. You'll see I have a point, despite the fact many of you have but small amounts of money. For two dollars each month, Heritage Manor Nursing Home could send a Bible through the American Bible Society to a remote outpost, somewhere in the world, in the language spoken in that area. There are more than forty residents here. It would require less than five cents from each for Heritage Manor to join the Bible-a-Month Club if everyone participated. Would you like to know you're having a *real* part in getting God's Word to the world? Is it worth sacrificing a package of cigarettes or a coke once during the month?"

Two weeks went by with no response whatsoever to my suggestion, and I felt downhearted about it. After the Bible study that day, while I was shaking the folks' hands (I shake their hands when I arrive and again before leaving), Mr. Hamilton said to Maxine, "Give her that dollar," pointing to me. Tears literally washed down her face as she reached into her billfold and handed me a lone dollar bill. I asked, "Mr. Hamilton, why do you want me to have this dollar?" "Because," came his reply, "I like the work you are doing."

I later asked Maxine if she cared to share with me the story of the dollar bill. "It was in his pocket," she said, "on the day he was almost killed, and I simply cannot spend it." I didn't know what I'd do with it but felt that I'd be led toward some worthy way in which to use it.

Only a few minutes after I received the gift from Mrs. Hamilton, Mrs. Revis called me aside. She too had some money for me, a tobacco pouch full of pennies. Mr. Thomas O'Brien had read my suggestion in the bulletin that they join the Bible-a-Month Club and wanted to contribute all the pennies he'd saved.

Remembering Mrs. Coyner's and Mr. Hamilton's gifts, I knew we could join the club; and I made the announcement to them. Residents, staff members, and volunteers got caught up in the spirit of what we were doing, and we sent *seven* Bibles as our first month's offering.

When those on the bulletin mailing list read the news, they too began sending us money with which to send Bibles. We have now provided, since May 1973, 721 Bibles. As long as a medium-sized nursing home can do such a deed, no one can dare say that God is dead.

Nor can anyone say that the ill and the elderly can no longer live creatively for God!

The work is hard, but I have good help. I am undergirded by my church and, to a large extent, by other churches in the community. Brother Trussell, the volunteer team, the employees at Heritage Manor, and Dr. J. W. Branch, Sr. do all they can to encourage me. I am welcomed when I go to the nursing home in a way that warms my heart.

Even so, for me to sing the Lord's song, to practice in my actions what I tell them to do, is hard work. Walking down the hall recently, I saw one whose head drooped as though he were asleep in his chair. A slight movement caused me to go on in. I was repulsed to see that his lips needed wiping and turned to walk on by. But the words "Inasmuch as ye did it not to one of the least of these, ye did it not to me" came to my mind. I went back and cleaned his face, a task his paralyzed arms rendered him unable to do for himself. He smiled and said, "Thank you, Teacher." I walked on then, feeling that I had given "a cup of cold water" in the Lord's name.

It was also hard to keep going to Mrs. Burns, lying as still and as silent as death—a vegetable, I'd been told—touching her and saying, "God bless you." But I kept going and one day, a few months later, she haltingly answered, "God bless you too." That was one of my life's highest moments—another reminder that, with God, there are no impossible dreams.

She regained her speech, hearing, and alertness of mind and is learning to walk. But her eyesight did not return. I have no better friend on earth than Mrs. Burns. She prays for me probably more than any friend I have. Prayer is a work she can do well.

As I became more deeply involved with the joys and sorrows of the residents, I grew to know their relatives and friends. This added a whole new dimension to my life. Many of my smallest deeds toward helping the ill and the elderly to again see themselves as a vital part of God's creative history reverberated into a glad realization that my own life had taken on a new meaning.

I'd been ministering to them for about a week when I realized I was coming to be known by a very special name. My first knowledge of this came about in a very heartwarming manner. I was walking in front of church one day when I heard voices exclaiming, "There's *Teacher!*" I couldn't tell where the voices were coming from and didn't even know I was the one being addressed. Walking on, I again heard *"Teacher!"* Then I noticed a pickup truck a few feet away and realized that the folks were speaking to *me*. It was the janitor at Heritage Manor and Mrs. Olivia Thomas, the "pure gold" housekeeper there. I was to come to love her with all my heart. She is one of the dearest people I know. One of them said to the other, "I *told* you that was Teacher!"

Shortly afterward I was visiting in a resident's room and heard a very impatient voice down the hall shout, "Will you *shut up?* I'm trying to hear what *Teacher's* saying!" (I had to speak rather loudly to many of them, and the others could hear me and really could listen to what I said.) I'd heard them announcing, "Teacher's here!" up and down the hall many times.

Mr. Harris' sons and daughters live in Omaha. As soon as he realized that I was not a phony, he asked me to write to them. Soon I was writing to and receiving letters from all of them, much to his delight. Mrs. Betty Jackson and Mrs. Ruth Conway each sent me a dollar one Christmas. I was deeply touched by the gesture and bought a small book that I shall always treasure. They still write and express their appreciation over and over for my interest in their father. His son Roy, also in Omaha, along with Mrs. Jackson, Mrs. Conway, and another daughter, Mrs. Mildred Holmes, have written, called, and visited me. Never in all my life have I known folks who responded more warmly to kindnesses than Mr. Harris and his family.

Mr. Louis Shaw, another of my black "pupils," wanted no "letter-writing favors" from me for many weeks. Sensing his fear that perhaps I wasn't sincere, I kept insisting that he name a relative to whom I could write for him. He seemed so alone that I really wanted him to hear from someone he knew. Finally he agreed that he'd like to hear from his niece, Mrs. Gertrude Criner, in Fort Smith.

I wrote to her, and soon afterward she telephoned me. I invited her to visit me, which she did. It was a stiff visit at first. She seemed afraid to hope that I really was interested in her uncle or her. After a while, however, her doubts and fears seemed to vanish away; and she broke down and wept for sheer joy. When she could talk she said, "Mrs. Alderman, I had been praying for weeks for some of my relatives in Hope to write me some news of my uncle Bubber (Bubber is his nickname), but none of them did. Then I got the letter from a lady of 'that group,' and I couldn't believe it was true. I went on my knees and thanked God for your letter, and I'll love you for as long as I live." That was the first time I'd ever heard white people referred to as "that other group."

Mrs. Criner and her sister, Mrs. Doris Parker, are good friends of mine now and remember me in their prayers.

And prayer is something I need a lot of as I go along in this work. A few years ago Mrs. Marietta Moses sat behind me one night at church and told me something I especially like to remember. "I want you to know," she said, "that there's *one* person who prays fervently for you *every* Wednesday morning." It was heartening to hear. Edwin often tells me, "Whatever I'm doing, I breathe a prayer for you at ten o'clock on Wednesday mornings." Dorcas' mother, Mrs. W. W. Kersh, is this kind of a faithful friend. The WMU prayer circle, directed by Mrs. Elizabeth Routon and Mrs. Sybil Watson, and my ever-faithful supporter, the Mission Action Group, directed by Mrs. Marie Gunter, are real "live wires" of help.

When a resident shouted, "I'm going to hell and expect to see a lot of other folks I know when I get there," and in the next breath shouted again, "and *you* take your flowers and get out!" it was mighty good to know those folks were praying for me. That's the only time a resident ever upset me so badly that I got angina pains.

When I told Dr. Lowell Harris about it, he reassured me by saying, "Rosalie, there's more hope that you can help him than if he held his feelings in." So I tried to be hopeful.

It was a gloomy November Saturday afternoon. He was a new resident who was in special need of encouragement. I gathered chrysanthemums from the yard and went out to see him, hoping to brighten his day a little. His tirade really upset me, and I got away from him in a hurry. I didn't forget him, though. I prayed for him and for me too.

Then I went back. That time I carried no flowers. I took my Bible. Pausing at the door I asked, "Sir, may I come in?" "Yes," he nodded. I continued, "Is it all right if I read the Bible?" Weeping, he again nodded yes. I told him how utterly needless it was for him to choose to go to hell when Christ had died to save him from that place. I just couldn't help adding, "And whoever else you may expect to see there, count me out because I'm *not* going to be there!"

The sick and the aged sometimes may seem to act like childish brats as they suffer the awful pangs that go along with adjusting to life in a nursing home. But they are *men* and *women*. And any of us, whether nurse, doctor, relative or volunteer worker, who doesn't treat them gently and with love and tenderness is committing a sin against them and against God.

It was not an easy task to lead this gentleman, whose health had slipped away and whose dreams had turned to nightmares, to believe that God loved him. Thankfully, however, it was done. Mrs. Revis and I worked long and hard with him and finally convinced him. But *only* after he realized that *we* loved him.

8
How Mr. Hamilton Met His Master

One Monday morning Maxine Hamilton called to tell me, "Rosalie, you'll hear about this, so I might as well tell you. Yesterday Bob spoke up and told a group at Heritage Manor, 'I just want to tell you this. I know now I'm going to heaven, and *when I get there*, I mean to leave *this wheelchair at the door!*'"

Initially, I felt shocked. Then there came to my mind the many times I'd heard him say, "God rose from the dead!" and "He loved me first, but I love him now." The full impact then of the very depth of his faith in his Savior hit me. Why, he was sure he'd not only go to heaven but that he'd also have a perfect body when he got there, no longer needing that hated wheelchair. And he simply said so—with a bit more emphasis than was necessary; but who would venture to say that God, who knows our frailties, did not appreciate the humor of the situation?

Picturing the shocked faces about Mr. Hamilton that morning and his own serious face as he apologized to them, I began laughing and couldn't stop until I was too weak to go on. I can honestly say too that I believe God laughed, from sheer joy and appreciation. I can also imagine hearing our Lord say to Bob on that occasion, "Your faith hath indeed made you whole."

One night in January 1975, Maxine called again. She was in deep trouble. "Bob," she said, "is seriously ill and in the hospital." I went with her to see him. He was glad to see us both. Never was a man more in love with his wife than he. Nor did one ever appreciate his Bible teacher more. I brought her home with me and gave her some supper. We took some cake back to him, but he didn't eat it.

He did thank me, though, for being there. A few nights later while I was sitting there with them as he slept, Maxine asked, "Rosalie, will you speak at his service?" God was undoubtedly very close by. Otherwise I'd have exclaimed, *"What?"* While I labored to get myself under control, she continued, "You are the nearest to a pastor he ever had, and I would appreciate it if you'd speak at his funeral."

I promised to do whatever I could, but I didn't believe he was dying and said so. It turned out she was right. Only hours later I was in the beauty shop when Mrs. Abby Breeding, who works at Herndon Funeral Home, came in and said, "Robert Hamilton died a few minutes ago."

My burden then seemed too much. Not only did my heart break in grief, but I'd promised to speak at his funeral. I wished then I'd not promised, but it was too late to wish.

I knew Maxine would be trying to call me and would desperately need me, so I returned home immediately and called her. I even dared to hope she'd made arrangements for someone to speak at the service. Someone besides me, that is.

She had not and quite soon got around to telling me so. And again I promised to do what I could, feeling a lot the way Abraham must have felt when "he went out, not knowing whither he went" (Heb. 11:8). I prayed earnestly for guidance, then called Dorcas and asked her to go with me to see Maxine.

I knew before arriving at her home that I'd have to speak at the service. It was a small deed I could do in return for the love I'd been shown, but I could not shoulder the whole service. At her suggestion I asked Brother Cecil O'Steen, who knew Mr. Hamilton's family, to speak. He readily consented. Dorcas agreed to sing a solo. She sang "Precious Lord, Take My Hand." Then I rose and spoke.

It was not as difficult as I'd expected it to be. With Dorcas, Betty Moore, and Rose Luck sitting on the front bench with me and Edwin in the congregation, I felt supported. Rose had been in the service at Heritage Manor on the morning that Mr. Hamilton professed his faith in Christ and mentioned how vividly she remembered this as we made our way out.

The comments made on the words I spoke were so touching that I was thankful I'd gone on and done my best.

I could never count the times we've all thanked God, even

as we've grieved over our loss, that Mr. Hamilton went to meet his Master clothed in garments of faith. And we'd been permitted to have a part in it all. We're also thankful for the sweet and intangible presence of that departed friend's love hovering around us. Just a few days ago Dorcas and I agreed, "Mr. Hamilton still seems very close by." We believe that he is because God is, and he is with God.

9
A Friend in Deed

I had been teaching the Bible, visiting residents in their rooms, and ministering in whatever way I could for months before the folks could bring themselves to believe I'd really be coming back. The last words I'd always hear before leaving were "Will you be back?" This puzzled me. Then Harry E. Dayton, a young student of pharmacy, and his mother, Mrs. Clara Dayton, visited in our home, and I learned why they were so concerned as to whether I'd be back.

Clara, a cousin of Edwin's, introduced us soon after she went to teach English at East Lincoln High School in the community where I lived outside Brookhaven, Mississippi. Through the years of our marriage we've been very close to her, her husband Harry who is a minister, and their son, Harry E. She had a lot of influence on my early Christian life. It was therefore natural that I should want her and Harry E. (her husband had died a few years ago) to accompany me to the nursing home.

She called me aside and said, "I'm sorry, but Harry E. won't go with us to the home." "Why on earth not?" I asked. "Because," she replied, "he once went with a BSU group from Mississippi College to visit in a nursing home. When they left the folks cried, and it depresses him to remember it."

I then said to him, "You come on. I guarantee that you'll see no one crying, and you'll not feel depressed." They went with me and took turns at playing the piano as I led the singing. Afterward I asked him, "Do you feel depressed over going?" "No, Aunt Rosalie," came his quick answer, "but I can tell you why! They *know* you are going back!"

That they might have wondered whether I'd be back just hadn't occurred to me. So I began working harder to assure them that I'd always be coming back.

I like to hope I'm making their hours less lonely by going to see them often. Anyone who goes daily into the room of a shut-in enables that person to have a reason for waking up each morning that's more gratifying than merely looking forward to the day's soap opera episodes.

Friendships are brought into being in that manner. We all need the security of having and being a friend, but the ill and elderly one who can no longer take care of his or her home or even remain in it desperately needs *real* friends. By a friend I mean one who is faithful to visit, call on the telephone, or write, when the shut-in is nice and pleasant to be around as well as when he is very *unpleasant.* He needs the steady "always-thereness" of the truly *faithful* friend who'll go to him with the attitude "But for the grace of God, I would be in that lonely room."

There was one little lady who never failed to rub me the wrong way. Without meaning to, I seemed to have a talent for doing the same for her. Thinking about that one night as I prayed, I realized I honestly did *not* like her and in the same breath asked God to remove the feeling from me. Soon I went back to see her, walking quickly toward her with no idea at all what I'd say or do but depending on God for an inspiration. When I reached her side I put my arms about her shoulders and said, "I love you!"

I don't really know which of us was the more surprised at my words. Her little careworn face began to glow with a light I'd never before seen in her countenance as she simply cooed, "Y-o-o-u d-o-o?" I did not know whether I was speaking truthfully at first; but after her eager response, I knew I was telling the truth when I said, "Yes, my dear, I do!"

And I've loved her ever since. She loves me too, a fact which has caused me a real problem a lot of the time. She never fails to reach her arms out and draw me to her in a hug. The problem is that she likes snuff, and the odor of it makes me quite sick if I'm close enough to it. I got alarmed one day when she put her face against mine. I honestly didn't know whether my stomach would tolerate the odor of her snuff. It so happened, though, that she smelled clean and sweet. She was out of snuff and wanted me to loan her some. When I told her I didn't use it, she looked at me sympathetically and said, "Well, don't worry. I love you anyway!"

She knows that I'm her friend and that I love her. How much does that count for when the little lady's mind seems to have deteriorated so that she seems unaware of just about everything else? It matters a great deal to me. Before I learned to love her and gave her the chance to love me, her face and voice reflected bitterness and despair. Now she smiles and is soft-spoken and mild. That's something I don't know how to evaluate. I only know there's a conviction in my heart that it's all well worth my time.

A nursing home resident has the same right as does any other person about deciding whether he'll accept your friendship. It's wrong to force one's attentions on another. I respect the rights of those I visit to say whether I shall enter their rooms. I was told a few years ago, "You'll not get in to see *her!*" I didn't, either. Not at first. I went back, though. That time she didn't jump down my throat—as long as I remained near the door. When I went the third time and asked, "May I come in a moment?" she tiredly consented, "Oh well, for *just* a moment." Her face showed pleasant surprise when, less than five minutes later, I smilingly took my leave.

I shall never forget how great it made me feel a short while later when she urged me to stay longer *and* even invited me back!

The very first one to urge me to stay longer with her was a lady who very soundly put me in my place one day. As I approached Mrs. Anna Brown's room, I heard her complaining about feeling badly. Like the rookie I was, I offered, "Now, honey, just remember how the apostle Paul said he learned to be content in whatever state he was in." To which she retorted, "And *you* just remember, young lady, that *I'm not the apostle Paul!*" I got out of her room in a hurry.

I also hurried back with my Bible in my hand and asked, "Would you like me to read you some of the Psalms?" She eagerly consented, begged me to stay longer, and urged me to see her often. I did. For as long as she lived. For as long as I live, I'll be thankful for the valuable lesson she taught me.

I'm glad to say that I keep on learning. One day while visiting among the folks, my sensitive ears along with a new resident's loud noises made an uncomfortable situation for me. I complained to Mrs. Smith about it. With a twinkle in her eye she said, "You know, when someone talks to him, he calms down." I took the hint. When I spoke to him his whole face turned into one nice pleasant smile. He so appreciated my brief gesture that I had the feeling God had especially blessed *that* small "cup of cold water in his name."

I like to remember an expression I heard Mrs. Martha Jones, a nurse, use one day. I was talking to her over the phone when I heard her exclaim, "Oh! I hear someone *needing* me!" I've thought of that expression many times. I've also prayed for a sensitive enough heart to *hear* whoever might be needing *me*— whether in my home, at my church, in my neighborhood, or at Heritage Manor Nursing Home.

It takes a person with a deeply sensitive heart to say and mean the words "But for God's grace, I would be in that lonely room." A heart that hears "between the words" will know when he who commands him *out* of his room is actually pleading "with groanings which cannot be heard" for him to also come back very soon. The well-tuned heart will be quick to pick up these silent pleas from the vast sea of lonely souls about him. And he'll find *some* way to brighten that person's life.

One lady was, to all appearances, simply unapproachable. This always concerns me deeply. In such a case I search for a sincere compliment to pass on. In her case, I mentioned her beautiful brown eyes. That didn't work. I was sorry about that too because she has *such* pretty eyes. I then looked deeply into those eyes and said, "I love you." She'd already begun a vehement argument against whatever I should happen to say to her but stopped suddenly when she heard what I said. It was almost as though she flinched. Not completely sure she had grasped my message, I touched her shoulder and asked, "Do you believe me?" A shy smile spread over her face then as she said, "Yes."

Saying and meaning "I love you" is one of the ways I can get her attention. Her other interest is the Bible-a-Month Club. She's intensely interested in that, contributes generously to it each month, and adores seeing her name listed in the bulletin as a supporter of that mission. (The names of each month's contributors are listed in a special bulletin.)

Here I am with the splendid staff of Heritage Manor Nursing Home.

A Wednesday morning Bible study in progress
(All photos courtesy of Clyde Davis)

Dale Middlebrooks reads the Bible to Mrs. Ruth Arnette, who is blind.

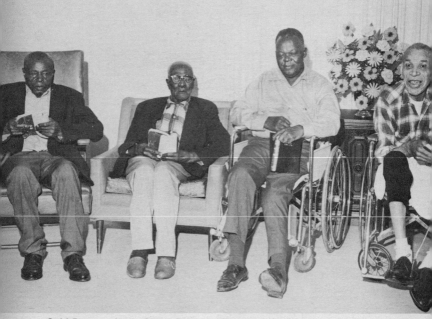
Gold Russaw, Louis Shaw, Osborne Chambers, and Ambrose Harris, who at first thought I was a "phony" (he's now with the Lord).

Mrs. Malinda Winberry, almost a century old, has her devotions.

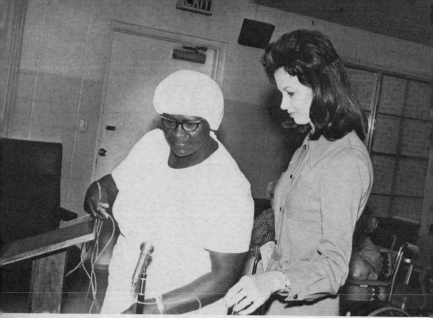

Mrs. Olivia Thomas, a faithful backer of the ministry, assists Mrs. W. H. Peterson, Jr., who sings for the services.

Mrs. Peterson leads the singing accompanied by Mrs. B. C. Hyatt, who was our pianist for six years.

Robert Hamilton became a Christian while at the home. He is now "at home" for eternity with Christ.

Mrs. Lucy Davis (left) reads with a former pupil, Mrs. Betty Moore. Mrs. Moore is our present pianist.

Mrs. Mae Bell Revis, supervisor at the home and staunch supporter

Mrs. Billie Russell, who has served as song leader

Dr. J. W. Branch, Sr., owner of the home, and Rev. Gerald W. Trussell

Mrs. Mabel Andrews, who led in providing a public address system for the hard-of-hearing, and Mrs. Rose Luck, chairperson of the Mission Action Group when I volunteered to teach at the home

Mrs. Myrtis Burns, at one time a vegetable due to brain surgery. Still blind, she prays for others while in her dark land.

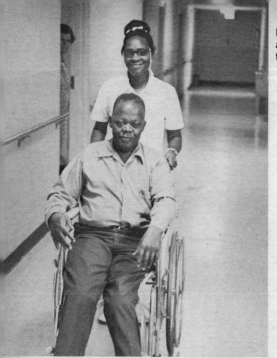

Mrs. Dorothy Walker, nurse's aide, rolls Osborne Chambers to Bible study.

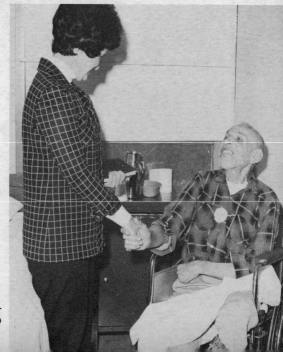

Ambrose Harris, shortly before he died, and I fellowship together.

10
More Reflections

As far as I know, what is being done at Heritage Manor Nursing Home here in Hope, Arkansas, is a pioneer work. Nowhere else on earth does a whole team of regular workers go each week to the same home and hold a religious service, where a member of that team is as close to the residents, to their families, and to the staff as a family member would be. I'm that person. Sometimes I go to see them daily. I'm called when one is ill or goes to the hospital. I visit them when one of them loses a loved one by death. I have received calls from the supervisor requesting that I talk to a resident about a problem. I go. Sometimes I feel that I help. At other times I don't really know. I'm sure of one thing, though. I do my best.

There was no precedent for the work. It was begun slowly and carefully—as some would say, "by ear." For a while I only read Scriptures, explained them, and tried to encourage these people to believe in themselves.

I believed active participation would bring about an increased interest in the Bible, and I encouraged them to join in praying the Lord's prayer at the close of each lesson. Soon afterward I began leading in the singing of hymns. Still later, I arranged a period during which they could say or read their favorite Scripture.

Very soon the Scripture verses became a real inspirational highlight of the meetings. The manner in which Mr. Henry Robinson said John 3:16 one day will long be remembered by us all. He said, "God so loved the world, that he gave his only begotten Son." His voice broke as he continued, "And that's more than any of *us* would do!" It was a deeply moving moment.

One of the first "verses" Mr. Hamilton said after acknowledging Jesus as his Savior was, "God loved me first, but I love him now." That was so meaningful to us. We knew he'd not been interested in the Bible until lately, but he was so caught up in its wonder that he meant to say verses whether he worded them exactly right or paraphrased them.

Mrs. Mittie Kelton had never said a Scripture for us. It occurred to me that she might do so should I urge her. Sure enough, she did. She still does that—when I single her out and invite her to.

The way in which Mrs. Orpha Johnson says her verse is particularly gratifying to us. Usually I'll ask Mr. Middlebrooks to take over that part of the service. Before I get to my chair and he reaches the podium, Mrs. Johnson begins saying her verse. Her eagerness makes us know she's enjoying what she's doing.

Mr. Osborne Chambers is an inspiration to us. Without fail he selects a verse from his daily devotional book to say or to read. Mrs. Bessie Mohon and Mrs. Vesta Williams usually read theirs.

Mrs. Willie Green does not read her verse—she can no longer see to read. But she quotes long passages to us. When she knew she was losing her sight, she spent much time memorizing the Bible.

Mrs. Lela Cox did not enter into this for a while but regularly does so now. The light that shines in Mr. Amon Whitten's countenance as he says a Bible verse he has loved for many decades warms each volunteer's heart. Other residents are also encouraged to put their discomforts aside for a while—long enough to look back down the years of their lives and recall a verse that was special to them.

I once dismissed a meeting after the Bible lesson, completely forgetting to have the Bible verses. I won't do that again. They remind me, "Don't forget our Bible verses," if I mention closing the meeting before this part of the service.

Hymn singing, the Lord's Prayer, and the Bible-verse period are still part of each Wednesday morning service. Other regular features are Mr. Middlebrooks' announcements of birthdays and other items of interest to the home, his Scripture reading and prayer, and Dorcas' solo, selected for its appropriateness to the subject for the day.

She usually selects the solo as well as the congregational songs. Sometimes, though, residents voice a request. They especially like "Amazing Grace" and "We'll Work Till Jesus Comes." The worth of our music program to the work could not possibly be estimated. A very elderly gentleman showed no interest at all in the service, other than to attend regularly, until the day we had music for the first time. On that day, as the soloist stood to sing, tears began trickling down this resident's face. I knew then that at long last, his heart had been touched.

That's not to say that the yardstick of emotion is what I judge the success of our meetings by. I suppose that in our meetings at Heritage Manor I have the feeling that "God's spirit beareth witness with mine" as to whether the service has been good. It's true that I see tears well up in a person's eyes from time to time, but I don't try to accomplish this. When it happens, it's my belief they're springing either from the memory of a long-ago experience or from a renewal of hope for the heavenly home that is now so much nearer than in times past.

Mrs. Lucy Johnson was an example of that. Her favorite hymn was "Pass Me Not, O Gentle Savior." The Bible verse she said most often was "Blessed are the dead which die in the Lord . . . that they may rest from their labours; and their works do follow them." Each time she said it, her eyes would become misty and her voice would tremble with emotion.

Mrs. Ethel Taylor's voice trembled too when she said her favorite, "I love the Lord, because he hath heard my voice and my supplications." I never hear the verse now without experiencing a sweet memory of Mrs. Taylor.

Our meetings are very short. I strive for what Dr. Paul Tournier describes as "quality experience" rather than "quantity activity." We work toward a *good* short meeting, one that holds attention till the last word is said.

Before the meetings, I work hard to condense what I mean to say to a short ten-minute talk which says a lot, and I have perfect attention.

Something that might bother a person attempting to establish and maintain work such as ours is that residents will sometimes get up and leave the room. At first this bothered me, but no more. They sometimes leave and listen to the singing from a distance away. Then they return, their nerves soothed.

I never pressure anyone to attend, and there has only been one who never once attended a meeting. Another Christian once told her that she shouldn't attend a meeting where a Baptist taught. Whatever that little woman's problem was, it wasn't lack of love. She loved me and often told me so. She also listened to me every Wednesday, but from the hall—never in the room with us.

One of the dearest friends I ever made at the nursing home was Mrs. Daisy Phillips, a lovely black amputee. On the first day that I asked the residents to quote their favorite Scripture verses, she sat and simply stared at me. As a matter of fact, that's about all *any* of them did that first day. I knew, though, that Mrs. Phillips could say Bible verses. She often quoted favorite ones when I visited with her in her room. So on the day while all were so stony silent (they just hadn't yet learned to loosen up), I said, "I reckon the cat got one lady's tongue because I *know* she can quote Scripture" and looked straight at her.

The next Wednesday at Bible verse time she said the whole twenty-seventh Psalm, straight through. Then, with an impish smile, she looked in my direction and said, "I don't suppose anybody would say the cat has my tongue *now!*" That fine woman's friendship enriched my life more than words could ever express.

Mr. Seth Crews gave me a real turn one day with a question. He asked, "Did you know my name is in the Bible?" to which I rather shamefacedly replied, "No, Mr. Crews, I surely didn't know the word 'Crews' was in the Bible." He said, "Not Crews! Seth!"

I then said, "Oh! I wasn't thinking about *that name.*" I decided then to enter into the spirit of what he was doing (we had quite an audience) and asked, "Did *you* know that Seth was Adam's son, that he lived to be 912 years old, and that he was the head of the geneological line that produced Jesus Christ?"

He didn't believe me. As I was leaving I heard him asking Mr. Middlebrooks to read him the passage where they'd find the "unbelievable thing I'd told them."

That was one of the lighter moments that sometimes come to us in the work. The ability to laugh heartily *with* the folks (never *at* them) is something that helps them and me, for brief moments at least, to forget some of the "other moments."

For some time now, we had been drawing near to one of those "other moments" which was to sadden us beyond measure—we could not ignore the fact that Mr. Crews was weakening very fast.

11
The People Need You

There came a Wednesday morning when Mr. Crews' voice was weak and his words so low we could scarcely make them out. Then the words "I love the Lord, because he first loved me," fell faintly on our ears.

I had a feeling that the words were a benediction. And soon afterward he was with his Lord "who had loved him *first.*"

Time, of course, heals grief. Or so we're told. But times of sorrow don't go by very fast.

It was the early fall of 1974. Dorcas' husband Pete was seriously ill. After the preoperative examination the doctor told her, "There is every indication that he has cancer of the colon. We will know for sure after the surgery."

She called me from the hospital and in as few words as possible repeated what the doctor had said.

The news stunned me. Dorcas is far more than a vital part of the new destiny God led me into. Both she and Pete are special friends of Edwin and myself. Pete and Edwin are fellow deacons in our church and often work on projects together.

I went out to Heritage Manor and shared the news with residents, staff members, and doctors. Many of the relatives of residents had become my friends. I called them too. To all I said, "Our beloved Mrs. Peterson needs our friendship now in a very special way. Her husband's life is in danger. You have appreciated her faithful work and have been lifted by the solos she has sung for you these many years. You know too that she loves you deeply.

"Now you have an opportunity to *prove* that you love her too. Pray that God might provide a miracle and restore her husband's health." I reminded them once again that prayer was a work that they were as well equipped to do as anyone else and as worthy a task as one could hope to be a part of.

I have never, in the almost seven years of working with the folks at Heritage Manor, been more grateful for their eagerness to "do what we can" than during that day and night of continuous prayers that they breathed in Pete's behalf.

When I returned home from the nursing home after asking that they "be at work praying" for the miracle we needed, I tried desperately to have the faith *I* needed. That was something I'd always had an easier time talking about than practicing. It seemed to me just then that I had a lot more fear than faith. But I prayed. How I prayed!

So did the people at Heritage. Mr. Middlebrooks, though sick himself, took his Bible into rooms and led in more prayer meetings than could be remembered.

I too went out during that endless day and prayed in rooms with some who could not so much as lift a hand. Nor could they speak except with their eyes. As I read the Bible's prayer-promises and told them the occasion for our prayer meeting, their eyes responded with what may have been a renewed hope that their work on earth was not yet done.

I hesitated to promise to go back and tell them the outcome of Pete's ordeal—I was frankly fearful of what it would be. But they deserved to know, even should the answer bring them sorrow. That was one thing they already knew a lot about. So I promised to let them know.

I came home and waited.

Even an endless day is somehow gotten through, and the darkness of what seems an eternal night cannot hold back a sunrise. The phone that's looked at for hours, with an almost unbearable dread, rings.

When I heard the lilt in Dorcas' voice, a surge of joy swept over me. I knew the miracle we'd prayed for had been granted. The malignancy, which had seemed such a certainty the day before, was miraculously no longer there.

It was a time to rejoice, to go out and share the glad news with the folks who'd cared enough to pray with all their hearts.

But even as we offered our prayers of thanksgiving for this blessing and before Dorcas could return to the work of leading the music for us, two other volunteer workers became ill. Mr. Middlebrooks had been in the hospital earlier for an appendectomy but had returned to the home.

Complications set in that rendered him unable to continue the many tasks he had been doing, which had been of invaluable help to me as I tried to maintain an effective ministry at the home. Without the help he'd been, the work was almost beyond my ability and strength to handle.

Then I got sick. It was really a matter of stopping long enough to recognize the fact that something was wrong. I didn't stop voluntarily. I collapsed. Mrs. Elizabeth Trussell (my pastor's wife) drove me to Shreveport for my checkup with Dr. Browning.

On this occasion, however, neither of those problems were causing my trouble. In answer to his query "What *seems* to be your problem?" I answered, "Nothing. Except if I eat anything other than sweet milk, my stomach hurts so I can't stand it."

"How long," he questioned, "has this been going on?"

"Only since mid-July." (It was then October 31.)

It's the only time Dr. Browning ever got mad at me. I don't even like to remember the look he had on his face when I told him how long my stomach had been hurting.

The lab reports, tests, and whatever revealed three areas of trouble. I was anemic. My blood sugar was low. Those inconveniences could have been corrected easily enough except for the third area of trouble. I had an ulcer.

I began taking the prescribed medication, four types in all. The pain in my stomach became sheer agony and did not subside until the medication for anemia and low blood sugar were discontinued.

For weeks I could neither teach at Heritage nor write the weekly bulletins for them. Brother Trussell faithfully went and did the teaching, but the folks missed their bulletins, which serve as their link to the world outside. They also missed being visited.

It was a time that tried my faith. Even when a few weeks later I could go and try to live up to what I'd taught them, I wasn't strong enough to drive my car.

Mrs. Rose Thrash, who has always been eager to help at Heritage in any possible way, would come by and drive me out. Then when Pete's condition improved enough for Dorcas to return to the work, she'd come by for me.

Still, the days and weeks were dark and discouraging. In the past, writing was something I could do to make an eternal night turn finally to day. Not now. There was too much pain to even allow me that amount of help.

It was on one of the worst of those dark days that I got a letter from Dr. Browning. Among other things which encouraged me, he wrote, "I know you are having a difficult struggle, but you are going to feel better. Remember these two things. First, the people you minister to *need* you; they're depending on you. Also, I am praying for you."

I was standing by the washing machine, folding clothes, as I read the letter and was so overcome I just lay my head down on the clothes and wept. His promise "I am praying for you" stirred what might have been a dormant faith on my part that I would indeed feel better again.

His words "The people *need* you" were echoed shortly afterward at Heritage. "Rosalie," Vera said, "Mama is real worried about you. She misses you and keeps asking where you are."

There were long-distance calls from folks in faraway states expressing disappointment over not receiving our weekly bulletins.

There's something about being needed that makes all the difference.

I got Dr. Browning's letter and read it again and imagined, for a brief moment, what it would be like *not* to be needed.

The thought reverberated into an anthem. All in the minor key. "Not needed." "Not needed." "Not needed." I lay my face on the arm of the couch after again reading the letter through and prayed. I knew I was needed, desperately needed, by the folks in the nursing home. With my mind still on the letter I'd just read, my thoughts went back to what had perhaps been the most desperate need I'd ever encountered in the work.

12
What Can You Know About Pain?

With only a few minutes to spare one afternoon, I went out to visit as many folks as I could before time to return home and get some supper together. I was going down the west corridor and had turned to enter a room on my left when I was stopped dead still by something I saw in the face of a woman who was a new arrival at the home.

When I looked into her face, I felt that I was seeing a picture of hell.

For a moment I was unable to move closer to her. Then, as if to complete the picture I'd already gotten, she threw the sheet back, revealing the most horrible sight I'd ever laid eyes on: a cancerous sore from which she'd torn the bandage.

By prayer and sheer willpower I managed to walk to her side and to touch her face with the tip of my hand.

Without even taking the time to introduce myself I said simply, "I'm sorry."

"Then *do* something!" she faintly hissed in answer.

"I wish I could, but I just can't."

"If you really cared, you could."

"I do care. It hurts me to see you suffer. I know your pain must seem more than you can bear."

It seemed then that I'd said a *very* wrong thing. "What can *you* know about pain? What can *you* know of my loneliness of being away from my family?"

I never felt more helpless in my life or more at a loss as to what to say. There are times when the answer is to say nothing, but I knew that was not such a time.

After a moment of just standing by her side and looking into her ravaged face, I said, "God bless you." I felt so ridiculous as I said it that I wondered just why I did say it. Even as I wondered, though, I heard myself say again "God *bless* you!" with an emphasis on the words which did not seem to come from *me*.

And, just at that moment, as complete a change as was ever written across the features of a human being took place in that "picture of hell" I'd been gazing upon.

An unnatural quietness was there.

I knew then that the emphasis on my last words had indeed *not* been mine, but God's.

We looked into each other's eyes a moment or so longer, neither of us speaking a word. Then I left her and returned home to prepare the supper which by now was to be a late one—I had stayed longer in the lady's room than I'd planned to.

I came away with mixed emotions over the experience. There was a strange feeling of peace. Mingled with it was a question which has haunted me ever since.

She had asked, "What can *you* know about pain? What can *you* know of the loneliness of being away from your family?"

The question that still troubles me is whether I had the right to deprive her of a story I could have shared with her—one that might have enabled her to feel less bitter about the loneliness of being separated from her family.

There is a longing on the part of the heartbroken person, the one who feels he has lost his family, to identify with a "kindred spirit." I had known times of pain that had seemed beyond my endurance; but the memory of it had dimmed enough that it would have been impossible for me to relate to that part of her anguish.

But I could have identified with her in the other sorrow she mentioned, that of being separated from her family. That tragedy crossed *my* path when I was still a child. And the memory of it has never dimmed.

I have an unshakable conviction that the experience was my first preparation for the new destiny into which God was to call me forty years later. For that reason I share it now.

13
I Lost My Family

My father was dead.

Only a few days earlier, I had heard him telling the family that I would look after them when he had to be away on overnight trips. It was as though his words were a magic carpet whisking me past my age of twelve years into an enchanted Grown-up Land.

Had I been thinking as a grown-up, I would have questioned his reason for entrusting the family to my care while Mother was still there. I also would have attached some significance to a look that passed between my parents at the time. Years later, I would remember that look and understand why they seemed sad at a time when I was so elated. They knew even then that, according to medical reports, neither of them could remain long with their children. They also knew that my feeling of happiness was to last but for a brief moment. Soon I would reel under the weight of burdens too heavy for my young shoulders.

Father went away a few days later, promising to return soon. I watched his departure with no premonition that he would never come back. He had never failed to return, usually within three days. I had been spared the knowledge that these trips were to see his cardiologist, and the nights spent in a hospital.

There is much work to be done on a farm, even during wintertime. I began mine with the eagerness of one anticipating the warm praise of an appreciative father.

Christmas was only a few days away, but the thought uppermost in my mind was the "well done" I expected to hear soon. The chores were not unpleasant. John, my eleven-year-old brother, gladly helped with all that was to be done, even when the task was to help entertain our four sisters, aged nine months to seven years.

My failure to notice we were having to care for them most of that day is understandable now. I was not a big girl, except in the realm of my imagination. The weather was warm and sunny, which was not unusual, even in December, for southern Mississippi. So we played outside most of the afternoon.

Not until I began gathering the children to go inside did I think of something vaguely disturbing. Mother had not come out once to see about us. This was so unlike her that I was gripped with a feeling of foreboding.

I went into the house by way of the kitchen, where she should have been preparing our supper. There was no sign of her having been there since noon. Something was wrong. I went toward her room and found her crumpled near the edge of her bed. I thought she was dead. She was alive but could hardly speak to me. After I had helped her into a more comfortable position, she told about the tragedy which was to end my childhood. She was so seriously ill that we were not to have her with us but for a short while longer.

I stumbled away from her and toward the door, sick with the realization of why I'd been asked to care for the family during my father's absence. My magic carpet crashed to earth. I was again a child but would no longer have a childhood. I wanted to fling myself into my father's arms again, and Mother had not been mistaken.

She was up some the next day, but a pall had settled upon the household. I kept from crying by thinking of how soon Father would be home. He would find some way to make everything all right again.

He didn't return on the third day, nor the fourth. On the fifth day I made a decision. I would ask my father not to make anymore overnight trips. I couldn't look after the family while he was away.

My decision to admit my feeling of helplessness gave me a feeling of peace. I answered a knock at the door with more confidence than I'd felt in five days. When I opened the door a neighbor said, "Mr. Givens contracted pneumonia. His heart. . . ."

I shall relate only two of the events that immediately followed. First: I was soon to realize that I must do what my father had said I should. I'd look after the family while he was away. Second: The minister who spoke at the funeral had a voice which sounded as though he were a sympathetic father attempting to ease the grief of his own child. From a vantage point of forty years, I look back and see that day in my life as a drama in which the great Script Writer was giving a father to one from whom he was also taking a father—I was to be adopted by the minister with the sympathetic voice.

Some of this minister's words, perhaps part of a prayer, seemed to drift around me and finally settle gently into my bruised heart. Like a wounded animal, unable to understand the reason for its pain, I gazed at the gray casket. "At Rest" was engraved on its lid, and I didn't like that at all. I was unable to believe that a man like my father could feel at rest while lying in a casket surrounded by a crowd of people. I felt profoundly sad and wished the casket might be moved from my view. It eventually was, and the feeling of emptiness was terrifying. I was to know the *real* depths of that feeling a few hours later, after we had returned home.

I learned that a house, furniture, land, and trees can seem to have vocal personalities. Our house had known laughter. Now it knew sorrow.

The shoulders of the mute musical instrument seemed to sag, for the strong hands which had made it come alive were no longer there.

The sewing machine, dishes, and stove communicated the message that the one who had taught me to use them would soon no longer be there to use them herself. Geraniums, ferns, and other plants seemed to droop with sadness, knowing the hands which tended them were growing weaker.

Land was not mere dirt. It was a field with a pulsating memory of one who had ploughed, planted, reaped, and once used a persimmon switch on me for not getting water to the field on time. Then he'd said, "I believe we'll sit in the shade and rest while you tell me what you have learned today." He glowed with pride when I said, "Mother is teaching me to sew now, for I'm not little any longer." I was six.

Trees were not objects to fill spaces in woods. They were as friends whispering their names, lest I forget Father's having taught me which was the white oak, maple, or sycamore. The many-splendored sweet gum he had described as being like a group of sisters—all in the same family but dressed in varied colors. On this hillside stood four of these sister trees. Last fall one of these had been dressed in red leaves. Another in orange. This one was brilliant yellow, and the fourth boasted leaves of dark green. On this bleak December day, though, they wore no colorful leaves. Their gray branches reminded me of the gray casket.

It had been decreed that the tall and stately southern pine should wear the color symbolic of life, even during the winter-time of death. But today it seemed quietly subdued as the wind in its branches moaned a melancholy ode to happier days when it had sighed in amusement concerning our never-ending argument over it. I had insisted it was a long-*straw* pine; my father always corrected me, saying it was a long-*leaf* pine.

Something he once did causes me, these many years later, to know he did his best to teach me how to cope with grief.

He brought me a young partridge whose mother had been killed. He told me that it could not live long but that he wanted me to care for it. I did as he'd asked; and when it died shortly afterward, I was brokenhearted. He helped John and me to have its funeral. When I began to cry he gripped my shoulder and said, "Now! Now! It won't always hurt this much."

But for eighteen months after his death my hurt had no chance to heal. I waged what was clearly a losing battle to hold together the family that I was to later see torn asunder.

Once when I was overcome by despair because of Mother's illness, I called out to Father for help, knowing he was dead and could not help me.

This frightened cry started me thinking about something I had witnessed in my father's life when I was about eight years old. He had stood near the altar of a church, tall, lean, slightly pale, promising to obey someone's commandments. It was confusing to me, as I couldn't imagine him obeying anybody. It was a habit with *him* to *be* obeyed.

Just then, as my heart was aching so for Mother to get well yet knowing that she never could, I began to realize that the one whom Father had promised to obey as he stood in that church was the Almighty God. I also felt that now it was my father's God quieting my breaking heart with the words "Now! Now! It won't always hurt this much."

Shortly afterward, when our money was all gone, I exercised a faith and courage—a memory which causes me to smile wistfully and which causes me to regret the "growing up" of that childlike faith and courage.

On that occasion, I simply told Mother not to worry. John and I would get a job and bring her some money. I then took John by the hand and went out to look for this job.

About a half-mile up the road we saw a house that looked friendly. As we made our way toward it, we saw a girl in the yard. Her brown eyes twinkled as she said, "Hi! What's your name and where are you going?" My very dignified answer was, "My name is Rosalie Givens, and this little boy is my brother John." (The fact that "this little boy" was only a year younger than myself didn't take away a bit of my feeling of being real grown-up that day.) "We are going to get a job because we don't have any more money at our house. What is *your* name?"

A warm smile spread over her face as she answered, "My name's Lucille Blackwell, and this is my house. Come on in!" So began a deep and satisfying friendship that has endured for over forty years.

We followed her inside where her mother, "Miss Mamie," as we were to lovingly call her from then on, was preparing a meal. The food smelled so good that we forgot all about our manners and stood before her looking as hungry as we felt. She naturally invited us to eat. And we ate! She and John and I then played until dark which *seemed* to come a lot earlier than usual.

I was so enchanted with my new friendship that I forgot, for a while, that I had no father. I had also forgotten to get a job.

Later, though, we found work with some neighbors who were genuinely kind. We helped them harvest tomatoes and cabbage and found our careers as young breadwinners fairly pleasant.

The next work we found, however, was not so pleasant.

About three miles further up the road, we found a job picking cotton. That was neither pleasant nor profitable. Neither of us could pick a hundred pounds in a day. And it was a lot different than taking water to my father in the field.

When this work was over, we had scarcely earned enough to buy school books for the four of us who went to school. I remember being glad the younger children did not go to school and would not need books.

We went to school with Lucille and her father, who was one of the teachers. Her brothers went along too. Since I had not gotten *that* interested in boys yet, there was nothing exciting about her brothers except my constant fear that the one named Toxie would put another frog down my back.

I was introduced to a Mr. Terry, one of the teachers at this school. I immediately loved him. He was the son of the minister who conducted my father's funeral. Though unknown to me then, this friendship between teacher and pupil was another link in the chain that held my future. I was to become his little sister and would love all his family for the rest of my life.

In the meantime, though, there were some sorrows to be borne.

The sands were running low on the time allotted for my family to remain together. Mother could be up less now. Once when I entered her room she was praying. She was also quietly weeping. When she became aware of my presence, she said, "Rosalie, you have been faithful to the charge entrusted to you by your father, and it has enabled me to be with you children a while longer. Someday, when you are a mother, you will know that this was the most wonderful gift that anyone could have given me.

"But the time has come when I must go into a hospital. I have arranged for you children to have homes where you will be protected and educated. Please remember always that an education is something you cannot be robbed of. Also, remember that you have been taught to be a lady."

By then her lips had become unable to form words. But her eyes talked on.

When she had finished talking, there was an awkward and

painful pause. I knew she wished that I would say something, and I wished I could. But I just could not.

Instead, I walked out of the house and almost ran to a nearby creek bank where I sat for a long time. I thought about trying to pray, but a noisy frog distracted me. I gazed in the direction of the noise and saw a sandbar where we had enjoyed one of the few carefree times we'd had since my father's death. We'd all waded, splashed water on each other, and laughed while searching for a wash pot that a heavy rain had swept from its place on the creek bank. We had found it on that sandbar with only a few inches of it visible above the sand. We excitedly dug it out as though it were a hidden treasure.

I fervently wished the hands of time would turn backward and let us laugh again while wading in a creek.

I wished they would turn even further backward to a time when Father came in from the field to ask why I was crying. I'd gotten hurt while playing. The significant part of the memory was that my father had come when I was hurt. I was hurting now as though a million knives were probing my heart. And no amount of wishing could prevent those hands of time from racing forward at a sickening pace.

Returning to the house, I paused to watch John playing an improvised game of "marble solitaire." For obvious reasons, he was using small hickory nuts instead of real marbles.

Watching him then, after Mother's talk had forced me to reckon with our inevitable separation, I saw more clearly just how small and defenseless he was. I'd always been there to defend him against larger children who teased him and called him a runt. (Although he grew to a height of more than six feet, he barely reached my shoulders then. It seemed I was *always* fighting off those who were trying to run over him.)

In such a short while, I would no longer be there. Who would protect him then?

As it turned out, nobody protected him. Nobody adopted the little boy who had no idea where his family was. He was to wander for ten lonely years searching for that magical "Somewhere," where he would again be part of a family.

Then an event which was undoubtedly another scene penned by the great Script Writer unfolded and placed him within a few miles of the home he had been looking for.

A man working beside him on a construction job told him about a newly married couple who had moved into that vicinity. This was of no particular interest to him until the couple's first names were mentioned. Then, in answer to a quick and breathless question from John, the man answered, "Yes, the girl does have *very* black hair. Why do you ask?"

More questions were asked and answered. A few hours later, my husband Edwin opened our door to a boy who was "wondering if my sister might live here." He had seen the grown-up young woman who stood just back of Edwin and knew he'd found his sister. What he didn't yet know was that he had also found a home. Edwin welcomed him into our family circle, where he has remained, never having married.

At the time, however, it was hard to wrest my attention from the boy playing marbles until a movement in the direction of the house caught my attention. Upon looking more closely, I saw my four little sisters huddled together on the porch. I walked on to the porch and sat on the top step.

My thoughts of Mother so ill inside the house, the boy outside trying to play marbles with hickory nuts, and the little sisters whose faces clearly indicated they knew something disturbing was in the air suddenly seemed just too much. I dropped my head into my hands and would have wept, but my little baby sister Lillian didn't give me the chance. She forced her way into my lap and rested her head on my shoulder. I held her closer than I ever had before, wondering if the other family, so soon to have her, would love her as much as we did.

The dawning of what was to be our last day together was not unlike other mornings—except that it was my birthday. Lucille and two other friends, Grace Hearn and Irene Boyles, had planned to surprise me with a picnic. Lucille baked a cake, and they met at our house about noon.

I was no longer there.

Shortly after breakfast Mother told us we would be going into different homes. She bravely bowed to a cruel fate and went about her duties to her children. Her only flicker of emotion was to hold her baby a bit closer. She was never to see that baby again. She died in a hospital, thinking she was alone, having lapsed into a coma before John and I could reach her. Years later, I was told of her grief for the children who, in her words, "are being cared for now."

Arrangements were complete.

By midmorning we were well into the last poignant scene of our family drama. By some ironic twist of fate, I, who was to have cared for all of us, was to be the first to leave.

When I turned to walk away, we were all gripped by a paralyzing silence. Then there was a frantic cry for me to wait. My little sister Annie was coming toward me with a bouquet of flowers she had picked for me. Reaching for them, I glimpsed the stricken faces of those whom I was leaving and desperately wished for the sound of my father's voice saying, "Now! Now! It won't always hurt this much." But there was no voice. No sound at all. Breaking hearts can be as silent as a tomb.

My last name became Terry. (It was changed back to Givens after the birth of our children, as I wanted my natural parents' names on their birth certificates.) I loved my new parents, brothers, and sisters. Bessie, one of those sisters, still seems very much like a mother to me.

Walter, a brother, was in the state legislature. After about a week, he suggested I go with him to Jackson to visit my sisters while he attended some business at the capitol. That was when I began loving him as I had his brother John, my beloved schoolteacher. A short time later I also loved Edith, the girl Walter married.

When we reached the children's home I was stunned to learn that only my four-year-old sister Minnie Ruth was still there. The others had already been placed, and I was not to be told where they were.

That visit with Minnie Ruth can only be described as stark and raw heartbreak. Amid piteous pleas of "Can't I go home with my sister?" she was torn from my arms and told she would have to stay there. She then wiped her eyes and calmly followed me to the steps where she sat and waved to me until I was out of sight.

I'd tried to comfort her and myself with Walter's promise to take me back to see her real soon.

He kept his promise. He took me back a short while later. But she was no longer there.

I was appalled by the loss of this one remaining member of my family. And before I was to see this four-year-old sister again, I would be a mother of a four-year-old daughter.

So began the years during which I had everything I wanted except the family I'd lost.

Years later I found Annie.

Still later, and in a way which sounds like pure fiction, I was reunited with my baby sister Lillian. Her parents found me!

I was invited to meet Mr. and Mrs. Joe Taylor and their ten-year-old daughter in the lobby of a Jackson hotel. They were already there when I arrived. When the four of us faced each other, none of us could think of anything to say.

Finally Lillian, who had calmly gone about looking me over, asked, "Is she my sister?" A day or so later she decided we were not sisters because "we're not quarreling like sisters."

I was soon convinced that the baby sister I'd loved and lost did indeed have a mother and father who loved her. (Lillian is now Mrs. Bill Rogers.)

About two and one-half years after I married, I received a letter from a former employee of the children's home telling of my sister Lucille's whereabouts and that it could be arranged for her to live with us. Again Edwin opened his heart and home. Lucille came to live with us and to go to school.

Years went by without my finding so much as a clue to Minnie Ruth's whereabouts. I went once more to the children's home to ask if they would only tell me whether she was still living.

I would hesitate to relate what followed that trip were I not able to verify it. A letter was there asking, "Does our daughter Minnie Ruth have a sister named Rosalie?"

Immediately afterward Mr. and Mrs. A. J. Hill of Hattiesburg, Mississippi, brought their nineteen-year-old daughter to meet the sister whom she had not seen since waving to her from the steps of the children's home fifteen years before.

How do you describe such a meeting?

She learned she had other sisters. And a brother John, then serving with Patton's Seventh Army in North Africa.

She remained for a long visit and spent a good bit of time looking at a picture of a handsome Air Force lieutenant, my husband's brother James. He is now a lieutenant colonel, still handsome, and has been married since 1945—to my sister Minnie Ruth.

The gathering into our home of relatives during the week preceding the wedding of our daughter Linda was a happy family reunion time for me.

During the happiness of those hours my father's words, "It won't always hurt this much," came to my mind. I was thankful that I could finally realize that he had spoken the truth.

14
God's Call

Only God and the person involved can fathom the depths
to which one sinks when he concludes that illness is to be his
"career" from then on.

There may be those who "enjoy bad health." As far back as
I can remember, I've heard that expression used to describe
some people. I can recall being amused when others would make
remarks about so and so "enjoying bad health."

I'd not be amused to hear it now.

I have a strong opinion on that subject. *Nobody* enjoys bad
health. *Nobody.*

There was never a more restless or a more miserable person
on earth than I was from mid-May 1966 until May 26, 1969.
That's the "era" of my "career" in bad health. By that I mean
that being sick, enduring pain, and going into hospitals were
my *only* activities. It was a living death as far as I was concerned.

And it was not just a matter of being *bored* sick with *being*
sick. I was bored, all right. I couldn't even remember what it
had been like to look forward to the next day.

However, the boredom all changed the moment I got God's
clear call to the work I'm now doing. The physical limitations
did *not* go away. I'd not dare leave home without nitroglycerine
and inderal in my purse.

Something that did happen was that I forgot what boredom
felt like.

It would be easy for one to think that my interest in life now
is due to the fact that I have a "hobby." It would be a desecration
of a holy God to call that work a hobby, a pastime, or a therapy.

It's none of those things. It's *work*.

I remember a person saying to me a few months after I began

going to Heritage, "I guess it's good in God's sight to try to comfort *old people* during their *last days.*"

After I got over being mad, I started laughing—to myself, that is. *"Old people."* The very idea!

There were and are people at Heritage younger than the person who made that silly statement.

"During their *last days*"—it's a natural enough assumption that anyone should think of a nursing home in those terms. But the image does not fit Heritage Manor Nursing Home in Hope, Arkansas.

Our going to them is undoubtedly a comfort to those who feel down and out, and many of them do have their share of bad days.

But I like to hope that the actual *work* that's done is in helping people who are either ill or retired or both to visualize the vistas of *real living* God still has in store for them.

Success does not crown all my efforts.

The saddest failure I ever had in the work was in not helping Mrs. Cora Crews to adjust to nursing-home life. She was the wife of our beloved Mr. Seth Crews. I met her at the nursing home on a Sunday afternoon, soon after I began visiting there. She was there to visit Mr. Crews.

After she and I talked a while, I told her I'd be glad to bring her with me each Wednesday morning to the meetings. She went along with me for years. I can still picture her sitting by Mr. Crews, straining to hear my words. Her hearing was not good.

She'd lived alone at her home for years, since Mr. Crews' health became too poor for him to remain at home.

One night she fell, broke her hip, and was hospitalized. Her recovery was not satisfactory. So in a few weeks she too went to Heritage Manor to live.

I have no regrets regarding my ministry to her during the first days of her adjustment period. I wish the story had ended that way.

Days began to turn into weeks without my sitting with her and trying to help her *want* to live. I didn't realize I was neglecting her, but I should have. I knew how she loved her home, the pride she took in doing things in her house. I should have realized she was going through a traumatic experience.

I did finally realize—too late.

She had gotten too weak to eat. I received a call to go and see if I could encourage her. And I tried. How I tried!

I'll never forget her plea, "Help me to have faith." They were the last words I heard her speak. A few hours later Mr. Middlebrooks called to tell me she'd passed away.

For as long as I live, I'll regret that I neglected her too long. She had a deep love and respect for me; and I could have influenced her, before it was too late, to eat her food, to even accept life in a nursing home.

I have forgiven myself. She would want me to do that. But I can't make the hurt go away. I can only hope that the sorrow of it will cause me to do better by the opportunities I yet have.

Nursing homes are a fact of life today. One of the most compassionate fields of service open to humanity is that of helping those who live in them. Going into one, from a home he has loved for a lifetime, is a traumatic experience which some are unable to cope with alone.

Helping them to make the adjustment is part of the work I do.

And, no, it really is not a hobby or a pastime.

What it is *is* work.

It's work that encompasses so much more than mere activity. There is such a love for the people that part of my work is to just go on and do my best, even when my heart is breaking.

I went by Branch Manor one day to visit with Mr. Harris. It's strange that I had no premonition at the time that my heart would soon break. As I look back to that afternoon, to the sheer joy of the fellowship we had, it seems I should have sensed something. But I didn't.

To begin with, he really told me off about something I'd done that he didn't like. (That's the kind of friends we were.) Since he had been moved over to Branch Manor to be nearer Dr. Branch, I did not see him as often as when he was at Heritage. I started in one day, though, forgetting it was the afternoon that they'd be gathered for the service Mrs. Marie Gunter and Mrs. Pauline Jackson would be having for the Branch folks.

When Marie saw me, she urged me to come on in; but I was

embarrassed at having barged in and got out as fast as I could. As I left I looked in the direction of Mr. Harris and others who had formerly been at Heritage and smiled. Then I waved and hurried out.

Later, on the afternoon I stopped by to see him, he said, "You didn't *do* us right the other day. Instead of staying with us, you just waved and told us good-bye. That made me feel *bad!*"

"Now, Mr. Harris, it wouldn't have been right for me to stay. Those other ladies were conducting that meeting."

"That's not so. *They* wanted you to stay too!"

"I'm sorry, Mr. Harris. I will come back. I promise you. I will even be the speaker for your meeting the next time I'm invited." (I'd been asked countless times to speak for them but hadn't done so.)

On my way to keep that promise, I went with tear-dimmed eyes. I walked into the room literally filled with people (Marie had told them I'd be there) and was as warmly received as I've ever been in my life. There was a deep quietness. The attentive manner in which they listened would have warmed any speaker's heart.

The ache in mine was too deep for me to feel the warmth about me. The wonderful friend I'd promised, "I'll come back and even be your speaker the next time I'm invited," was not there to smile the welcome to which I'd become accustomed.

On the afternoon that he told me off, he also forgave me—but not before I promised to teach for them sometime. He had begged me to "come over here and teach us" ever since he'd gone to Branch Manor. I'd also been invited several times by the staff, but I didn't (and still don't) see how I could take on more than the Heritage Manor work.

That afternoon he asked me about all the Heritage folks. "I am worried," he said, "about Maxine." (This occurred shortly after Mr. Hamilton died.) I told him I'd remember him to her. He asked me about Edwin.

"Does he still have all those chickens—a hundred thousand of them?"

"Yes."

"That's some *bunch* of chickens!"

"Yes, sir, it is."

"Teacher, I sure do love you."

"I know you do, Mr. Harris."

He looked intently into my face then and said, "Teacher, I sure do thank you for making me stop hating white folks."

"I didn't do that, Mr. Harris. God did."

"Well, he *didn't* do it till *you* started teaching me!"

The way he was speaking concerned me. I said, "Mr. Harris, please don't talk that way. It sounds like you are blaming God for something, and that's wrong of you."

Again he looked intently at me. For a moment he considered what I'd said. Then the most radiant smile spread over his face as he said, "You sure are right!"

For a moment or so neither of us spoke again. Then he said, "Teacher, do you still call my name when you pray?" (I could never count the times he asked me that.)

"Mr. Harris, I not only call your name, but I pray for your family too."

I suppose that caused him to think of a member of my family he almost worshiped, for he then asked, "When's Mark coming?" (Mark Horn was my four-year-old grandson.)

I told him Mark would be coming in about two weeks. He smiled and said, "You be sure and bring him to see me." I knew Linda was planning to take Mark to see him and told him so.

Tears then began to fill his eyes a few moments later, as he asked if I'd pray for him. I prayed. He joined in and prayed too.

When I turned to leave, he wept again and asked, "When are you coming back?"

"Tomorrow," I promised.

Before I reached the door he asked, "Are you sure? You *are* coming back tomorrow?" I walked back to his bed and said, "Mr. Harris, you can count on it. I will be back tomorrow."

I left then. But I couldn't get him off my mind. He had never wept in my presence before except the time he'd bragged to me, "Mark called me by my name!" And though we'd talked about prayer many times, he'd never before asked me to pray in his presence.

That night was prayer meeting night at church. I felt I should ask that he be remembered and did so. I kept on praying for him until I went to sleep that night.

I went back as early the next day as I could. Marie met me and told me he was dead.

He'd had a coronary.

I'm still unable to remember the sorrow of that news without weeping. A dear friend, Mrs. Carolyn Lindsey, lab technician at Branch Hospital, saw me and invited me into her office. I'll always be grateful to her for helping me over some bad moments.

I went and told the folks at Heritage.

I returned home then and called Dorcas and Betty, who were as heartbroken as I. Betty went with me over to see Mr. Harris' family.

Edwin, knowing the depth of my grief, called to tell Linda. It would have been cruel not to tell her, as she was already making plans to take Mark to see him.

I had not been home long before the phone rang. Mr. Harris' daughter, Mrs. Betty Jackson of Omaha, Nebraska, was calling for me. "Mrs. Alderman," she asked, "will you speak at Daddy's funeral?" I'd just have to trust him to help me in this case, as he had when Mr. Hamilton died.

I am neither a women's libber nor a non-women's libber. I guess I'm just a woman. I have no quarrel with those who would disagree, but I just can't like the idea of women in pulpits.

When I volunteered to minister to the people at Heritage Manor, it never crossed my mind that I'd ever be asked to speak at a funeral.

I could not have refused Maxine. Nor could I refuse to help Mr. Harris' family.

I called Mrs. Jackson back to ask if she minded my asking Brother Trussell to help with the funeral. Before I could ask she said, "Daddy loved Brother Trussell so much. Would he speak too?"

I've been asked, "How *can* you go ahead with such a work, knowing there'll be more sorrows to bear?" It's not a bad question. I've asked it of myself at times.

15
My Messages

I believe the answer to the question as to how I can continue the work is in the fact that I try to live by the words the Lord said just before going back to the Father. He said to his followers: "Go ye therefore, and teach all nations, baptizing them in the name of the Father, and of the Son, and of the Holy Ghost: Teaching them to observe all things whatsoever I have commanded you: and, lo, I am with you alway, even unto the end of the world."

I know that I am called, as surely as anyone ever was, to do the work I'm doing—which is all that's mentioned above except to baptize. I'm happy enough to try to lead the lost to the Lord and do my best to be of some comfort to the many who need comfort.

I'll never stop missing Mr. Hamilton. But I never think of him without thanking God that I led him to a belief in Christ before he passed away. That goes a mighty long way toward helping bear the sorrow that goes with the work.

One phase of the work that sometimes seems more than I can continue with is the writing of a personal message for the weekly bulletins. These bulletins are mailed to the relatives of the residents. Each message is meant to encourage and to inspire the residents to keep their courage up and to hold onto their determination to live for the Lord, even in a nursing home.

It's hard work.

Is it worthwhile?

Yes, in many ways. It is their "newspaper." Their names appear in it when they have visitors and when they contribute to the Bible-a-Month Club. Residents know the bulletins are mailed to their relatives. The fact that a relative often reads a reference

I made to a resident gives that resident a feeling of pride.

They do many things that merit respect, and I do my best to relate this. It helps them to think of themselves in terms of being men and women of dignity, still in the stream of life, not as inanimate "things" whose *real* living is a thing of the past.

There are those who cannot hear but who can read. Were it not for the bulletin, they would have a feeling of being on the outside. The messages are my only means of teaching them.

My first real awareness of this came when Mr. Thomas O'Brien made his contribution to the Bible-a-Month Club. He was the first one to actually heed my efforts through the bulletin to interest the other residents in giving to this mission.

It was also about then that he let me know in some pretty plain language. "I don't appreciate folks not visiting with me just because I can't hear! I can talk."

His remarks were not directed at me, but they did remind me that I could do a bit better about visiting with him; and I tried to do that. The significant thing, though, at the time he gave the money for the Bible ministry, was the fact that he never would have known about it except for the bulletin.

There are times when a resident or someone dear to one has a deeper need than usual for intercessory prayer. I mention it in the bulletin. Those who have these special needs are encouraged to know that the people who read their "newspapers" are praying for them.

Something even more important than the good feeling a resident has over being remembered in the prayers of so many is that God *answers* prayers.

Mr. Middlebrooks became seriously ill again in the summer of 1975. He was so depressed he could not eat and got no better even after weeks in the hospital. Hundreds read the prayer request and remembered him daily. He got so much better that he says he doesn't even feel like the same person.

At the time of this writing, 721 Bibles have gone out to all parts of the world from Heritage Manor Nursing Home. In addition to the contributions of the nursing home residents, money comes from far and near, from readers who would otherwise not be contributing Bibles.

Who can estimate the worth of 721 Bibles in the hands of people who formerly had no copy of the Scriptures?

Sometimes, when a message is to be written, I can't do it, or so it seems. It's then that the miracle of what prayer can do is learned anew. In that way the writing, however difficult, is something that's good for me.

There's an old hymn entitled "Oh Love That Wilt Not Let Me Go." It's an apt description of the reason that keeps me going at this particular task that gets too tiresome at times. Residents and staff members alike get on low limbs and need all the encouragement they can get. They all tell me repeatedly that it helps them to read their "news." It's my love for all these folks that won't let me let go. Whatever I can do to make their work a bit easier to do is something I think of as my responsibility.

Following are copies of some of the messages:

Painful Choices

Knowing the pride Dr. W. H. Browning, a prominent Shreveport physician, had in the herd of registered cattle on his farm, I was understandably surprised to learn he was selling them.

A habit, often described as one causing "fools to rush in where angels fear to tread," led to my thoughtless question "Doesn't this hurt you?"

He'd been caught off guard; and, before he could mask it, the hurt was there in his expression. I wished then I'd kept quiet but couldn't help going on to ask, "Why are you doing this?"

His answer, so simply stated, was to become something akin to a standing-on-hallowed-ground experience to me, encouraging me to probe more deeply the underlying reasons behind choices I'd make.

In a voice subdued but resolute, he said, "It's difficult to hire adequate farm labor, and I must choose either keeping the cattle or keeping my medical practice. And the medical practice is something I will not give up!"

I was deeply moved, knowing he'd chosen in terms of what he could do to meet humanity's needs. Being a wealthy man, he didn't need the money from his practice; but he knew he was needed by other people. And, to borrow a line from one of Robert Frost's poems—"That made all the difference."

The meaningful life, by eternity's standard, demands choices that more often than not are painful. I looked once into the face of a young man in the throes of an agonizing choice and was awed to hear him say, "This is not what I want, but what I want isn't the important thing."

He'd spoken a profound truth. Jesus made the most agonizing choice in the history of mankind as he prayed in the garden of Gethsemane, "Father, if thou be willing, remove this cup from me: nevertheless not my will, but thine, be done."

It's understandable how the blind, the ill, and the lonely among you might pray to go on to heaven. If you feel this way, I do not condemn you. My heart goes out to you. Will you try, though, as you wait, to pray for someone who does not yet know Christ as Savior?

That choice would be difficult and painful. But it would also be rewarding.

God's Scales

I believe we all should pause once in a while along the rushing thoroughfares of our lives below the surface of our noise-filled hours. We should pose the question "What does my life amount to, anyway?"

The question should never be an outgrowth of anger, grief, discouragement, or despair. It should come out of an earnest desire to know ourselves as we really are to the end that we allow God to purify our motives and enable us to live our lives with purpose—*real* purpose, in terms of eternity.

It's necessary that we should find and acknowledge the real self which lives within each of us—somewhere amid all of our clutter and make-believe. Only then can we recognize that some of our activities are empty and worthless—from God's point of view, that is.

The Bible says, "He weighs carefully everything you do" (Prov. 5:21, TLB). Our "empty activities" will avail us nothing when weighed on God's scales.

This fact should prompt each of us to look again at the question "What does my life amount to, anyway?" In God's sight, does it have purpose? Or do I merely drift downstream with the currents of circumstance?

He who looks at that question seriously and dares to recognize what he sees is likely to find that much of his life is not as meaningful as it might be.

We should be encouraged, however, if in our self-searching we find some areas of emptiness. It's when we see and acknowledge our failings and take them to God in prayer that we can hope to build more useful lives.

The meaningful existence is not something reserved for a privileged few. Nor is the opportunity to live gloriously withheld from the ill person who gets about only by wheelchair. Two of the finest people I know pass their days in lonely rooms in nursing homes. One is in a wheelchair. Both are blind, in ill health, and unable to do much that we take for granted. But how they love! When I'm in their presence I feel a strange and healing warmth. Love is something that will not be found wanting when weighed in the balances of God's scales.

No one lives a meaningless life—or goes to meet the Lord empty-handed—who engages in faithful, consistent prayer. And that's something anyone can do: the old and the young, the healthy and those who travel by wheelchair, and even those who don't leave their beds.

The ultimate answer then to the question "What is my life worth, anyway?" is determined by the measure of one's desire to live worthily. So let us love God, love one another, and pray faithfully. In so doing, we'll have nothing to dread when the time comes for us to be weighed on God's scales.

I think of the residents and what the bulletins mean to them. I think of their families and how good they feel when they get news of the residents. Then some of the tiredness from it all just sort of fades away.

16
Hearing with the Heart

Another especially hard part of the work that often saddens me is my inability to communicate with some of the residents. I've learned a lot, though, in nearly seven years of working with some who cannot talk.

Some of the sweetest memories I have of the work are of some who could not speak audibly but who "talked" to me in other ways.

Mrs. Pauline Frazier's (and Mrs. Virginia Tate's) mother, Mrs. Emma Beard, was terminally ill. I went to see her almost daily, during which time a deep and mutual love grew between us.

She was very concerned about me when I got sick and had to go to St. Vincent's Hospital in Little Rock.

When I returned I went immediately to see her, but she'd failed so by then that she could no longer talk.

As was my custom when I was with her, I read Psalms 23, 90, and 91 to her and prayed for her.

When I turned to leave she became upset and made sounds of distress, which was an indication to me that she'd wished to hear something I'd failed to say. I went back and stood helplessly beside her for a while longer but could not think of what might be troubling her. I turned again to leave. That time her sounds of distress were increased.

Again I went back to her side, silently pleading for God to make me aware of what she wanted. Suddenly I knew. "Mrs. Beard," I said, "I understand you now. You want to know what the doctor in Little Rock told me.

"I'm very thankful to tell you that he promises I'll get better if I take care and do as he says." She smiled then and indicated that it was all right with her for me to leave. A few days later she passed away. I'd lost a real and dear friend, but she left me a legacy—a sure knowledge that love can and will find a way to communicate, regardless of how humanly impossible it may seem.

I went into Mr. Ross Crank's room. There I experienced the feeling of helplessness again. He too was terminally ill and seemingly unable to communicate. He made no sound at all. I started to go on out, but something—or Someone—caused me to go back to his side and read the twenty-third Psalm, though there was nothing to indicate he would know what I was doing.

Again I learned something. Before I'd read more than two or three verses, he stirred and made a sound. It was so weak I'd not have heard it except for my above-average hearing ability. I looked more closely into his eyes then and knew beyond any doubt that he was being comforted by the words I was reading to him.

Soon afterward he went on into eternity. He too left me with a gift I'll always treasure: an even stronger faith that God's Word indeed does accomplish its purpose. Nobody ever reads it in vain. I feel a strange and sweet comfort as I remember the experience with that fine man. And I thank God that as Mr. Crank lay dying, the words "Yea, though I walk through the valley of the shadow of death, I will fear no evil: for thou are with me" kept him from feeling alone.

I went out to the nursing home one morning just to visit around for a while as I often do. A new arrival was absolutely and utterly beside herself. Nothing I could say reached her. But I tried. I tried with all the strength I had but failed.

As I left I said, "I will be praying for you. And now may God bless you." I returned home then, burdened and sad about her. But I kept on praying.

The next day was Wednesday, the day of our meeting at Heritage. That day I saw a miracle which will, for as long as I live, strengthen my faith in prayer.

She was there, sitting only a few feet away from where I stood to teach. She literally drank in my every word in an attitude which made me know she accepted every promise God was making to us all from his Book. The expression on her face gave me a feeling of strength and peace.

She had a coronary at ten o'clock that night and died instantly.

I like to hope that the words from God's Book she'd heard, only a few hours earlier, were on her mind and in her heart as she went into the strange and mysterious "chambers of death."

Another lesson I learned about those who seemingly cannot be communicated with came from Mrs. Martha Folsom, one of the finest Christian women I ever knew. The lesson she taught me was thorough. I was unable to stop thinking about what she said to me until I wrote the following message for the bulletin:

Hearing Hearts

My keen sense of hearing was a real problem to our daughters Linda and Libby during their teen years. Regardless of where I happened to be about the house, they could only say things on the telephone to their boyfriends that they didn't mind my hearing. They quite often lamented to each other, "Mother can hear what we say before we even say it!"

The sense of hearing is one of God's richest blessings. It enables one with a sensitive ear to pick up runs in music and to hear them blending with the louder notes in a composition so clearly that the experience often moves him to tears. But there is no virtue whatsoever in hearing especially well with *only* our ears. If our hearts are dull and insensitive to even an unuttered cry somewhere about us, it's a sign that our hearing is impaired, regardless of what our ears might register in a test.

One *should* hear with the heart.

The poignancy of this truth was pointed up to me some time ago by Mrs. Martha Folsom. She had recently moved into our Heritage Manor "Family" and was feeling lost and disoriented. I was talking to someone near her but addressing no remarks directly to her as she didn't appear to be aware of what was going on around her. She did a pretty fair job, however, of teaching me not to think that way ever again.

"Young lady!" she stormed at me, "I wish you would hear *me.*" Being a grandmother myself, it was pleasant to be called a young lady; but the tone of her voice suggested that the way she was feeling toward me just then might be less than complimentary. I quickly went to her side, knelt down and took her hands in mine, and asked, "Honey, what is it you wish me to hear?" She was so taken aback that momentarily she could say nothing. Then she smiled and answered, "There is a great day up ahead." It was my turn to be speechless for a while, after which I quietly said, "Mrs. Folsom, I appreciate your reminding me of that." At that her eyes filled with tears and she said, "And I thank *you* for saying you *appreciate* me."

That dear little lady never fails now to say something nice to me, and there is no way to tell just how much encouragement this is. I find it interesting to recall that her first words to me were in the nature of a sound reprimand which I richly deserved. Her scolding and later sweet response to my interest have lingered with me and caused me to try to have a heart that hears well, especially so in cases where no sound is uttered—that's often the time when one needs most to be heard.

There is a deep need for "hearing hearts." There are those all around us who are hungering to be told they are appreciated, whose lives can be made worth the living by the person whose heart can hear their silent plea to be recognized as human beings. Let us try very hard to teach our hearts to hear; the day will surely come when we will want to be heard ourselves.

Mrs. Folsom's health got so much better, thanks to God and Mrs. Mavis Smith's refusal to give up, that she can communicate with me in a way which never fails to inspire and encourage me.

I stopped at the door of a little black lady's room. She lay so still and so quiet that I didn't think I should go in. I did, though, and touched her shoulder, very lightly so as not to startle her in case she was conscious. (I'd not seen her before and didn't know whether she might be in a coma.)

She quickly turned toward me, smiling and making sounds but not words. I later learned she'd had a stroke. Although she cannot say a word, her eyes tell me she loves me and wants me to visit her.

It may be that the lesson Mr. O'Brien taught me about the importance of my working at the task of communicating will be my most unforgettable one.

He got mad at me. Really angry. He quit contributing to the

Bible-a-Month Club and stopped coming to our meeting.

Not knowing he was mad at me, I went to his room to see why he wasn't sitting in his usual place one Wednesday morning. He told me he wanted to talk to me. I wrote (remember he cannot hear) that I had to go on and teach just then.

"Can't you come back here afterward?"

"Yes, sir, I will, but won't you come on out to the meeting?"

"I'm not going back out there until I get some answers!"

"All right, Mr. O'Brien, I'll come back as soon as the meeting is over."

When I returned to his room, I picked up the tablet he keeps handy and wrote, "Mr. O'Brien, I now have time for you to talk."

It was then that I learned he was mad at me. He showed me a bulletin message in which I'd written someting to the effect that I tried to minister to folks who were lonely and discouraged.

"I am *not* lonely," he said, "and I am *not* discouraged."

Needless to say, I was taken aback; but I had a ready and truthful answer. "Mr. O'Brien," I said, "I did not have you in mind when I wrote that. You are an unusual person in that, although you cannot hear, you read all the time, watch ball games, and mix with people.

"If I'd been aware of the possibility that I might hurt anyone's feelings, I'd have mentioned in that message that not all the residents at Heritage Manor are lonely and discouraged, but that many of them are.

"And a good many *are very lonely and very discouraged.* Just days ago a lady said to me, 'I am so lonely that I feel at times that God does not even hear me.'

"I apologize for hurting your feelings. I love you and would not have intentionally done that for anything. Now will you forgive me?"

"Yes," he said, "but I want to know why they quit acknowledging the money sent for Bibles. There used to be mention in the bulletins as to the money being received. I don't believe the money is going for Bibles."

"The American Bible Society does acknowledge the gift," I answered. "I just failed to mention the fact in the bulletin, not realizing it was necessary. Mr. O'Brien, that's an omission on my part that I promise will be corrected. And if you doubt the money is being sent, I can bring you my cancelled checks to prove it."

"I don't *want* to see your checks" he answered. "I never doubted your sending it. I just didn't see why they quit acknowledging it."

Again I said, "They did not quit. The American Bible Society sends receipts every month. I will see if I can find some of the correspondence from them and bring it for you to see."

I could see he was still upset, and I began to feel that way myself because it seemed I was getting nowhere.

"Mr. O'Brien," I continued, "I don't seem to have been any help to you today, but I want to say again that I love you dearly and have done my best to help you see that the things bothering you were not things I meant to happen. I am very tired now; and since I can't seem to help you, I must go on home."

"Yes, you have helped me. I understand better now and want to thank you for taking the time to explain it all to me."

How wonderful it was to know I had won my dear friend back. I gripped his hand and asked, "Are you coming back to our meetings now?"

"Yes," he smiled, "and I do appreciate your coming and talking to me."

I returned home exhausted. My right hand ached from all the writing I'd done to try to help him understand the things that had him worried. But it was worthwhile, a thousand times over. I'm still thanking God that Mr. O'Brien communicated his need to me and gave me a chance to help him.

When I arrived home I went immediately to search for one of the American Bible Society's "acknowledgments" that I felt pretty sure I'd find. I found one, typed him a letter explaining it, and went back out and took it for him to see.

The receipt read, "Thank you for your gift received for September '75. Your gift this month helps supply the spiritually hungry people of Pakistan with Scriptures."

I'll always regret having failed to copy the words in the bulletins, as the omission caused this dear friend (and myself) some real distress. Needless to say, I'll never make that mistake again.

When he read the acknowledgment, his face lit up as he said, "I just can't tell you how many times I read about that Pakistan flood." He didn't say so, but I knew he'd contribute to the Bible-a-Month Club at his very next opportunity.

17
Getting in Touch

In relating the problems (and blessings) that cross my path as I try to communicate with some who, because of physical impairments, are difficult to talk to, I've noticed something that I think is significant. The word *appreciate* has appeared more than a few times.

When I say I appreciate something or someone, it's a way of saying I am thankful. I think that has been the case with the people who expressed appreciation for my efforts to understand and communicate with them.

This fact came to my mind a few days after I went out to take the Bible-a-Month material for Mr. O'Brien to read. I was looking over the information and decided to read it myself. (I'm like all other busy people—often too rushed to do more than merely glance at words I should read closely.) I read a plea for more Bibles for spiritually hungry people in Pakistan.

When Mr. O'Brien read the news about Pakistan's desperate need for Bibles due to the flood that devastated their land a few years ago, he was moved and told me how much he appreciated my going back to help him understand.

After I read it, I found myself wanting to say, "And I thank *you,* Mr. O'Brien, for influencing me to look more closely at something that merited my attention." I could hardly wait to thank him again for his courage—I don't imagine it was easy for him to tell me how displeased he was with something I'd done (and something I should have done, but hadn't).

He has proven in many instances that he cares as deeply for "Teacher" as she does for him.

Once when I was in the hospital, I missed a couple of Wednesdays. On the morning of my first absence, Dorcas thoughtfully remembered that he'd be upset at not seeing me and wrote him a note explaining where I was. (There's a great deal of extra work in communicating with one who cannot hear, but the result is more than worth the effort.)

She forgot to write to him the next Wednesday morning. She said to me later, "I saw him struggling up from his chair (he can walk only by using crutches) and going back toward his room and wondered why. After a while I saw him coming toward me with his tablet. When he got near enough, he held it out and said, 'Tell me how she is!' "

On the Tuesday night following the experience where he "had to have some answers," I wrote my usual letter to him. (Since he cannot hear, I always take a letter to him on Wednesday morning.) In it I expressed my appreciation for his calling my attention to the problem which had been bothering him. I told him (truthfully), "Otherwise, I'd not have known. And I cannot help with a problem I'm unaware of."

I went especially early the next morning so I could give his letter to him and perhaps persuade him to attend our meeting, in case he'd changed his mind after promising to come back. His door was closed. *Never* had I seen his door closed before! I turned sadly away, trying real hard to hold back the tears. But I just couldn't help crying, knowing he'd closed his door to make sure I'd not go in to see him before the meeting.

I walked on to the dining room to shake hands with the early arrivals, and Mr. O'Brien was the first person I saw. *He* was one of those "early arrivals" that day. I was so overcome that I cried again, but I let it appear that I was having a problem with hay fever.

Communicating with Mrs. Daisy Phillips was never a problem until once when she was quite ill. When I reached the door of her hospital room, her face was turned toward me; but she gave no sign that she recognized me.

It appeared that she was too ill to know or care who I was. I was heartbroken because she and I loved each other dearly. I could not bring myself to leave her without doing all I could to make her know it was me, her "teacher," trying to talk to her. She was apparently too sick to reach.

Then I thought of something: her favorite Scripture, the

116

twenty-seventh Psalm. I began reading it to her. I stopped after the fourth or fifth verse, as it seemed I was only reading to an empty room. I was mistaken.

"Read the *rest* of it!" she commanded. It was an order I obeyed while thanking God for the blessing that comes my way on occasions when I refuse to give up.

I have no unique "gift" for establishing lines of communication between these people and myself, except for the honest and sincere love I have for them and the stubborn refusal to give up trying to help when they have a problem. My experience with Mr. O'Brien causes me to hope that this may be all that's required.

Communication with nonspeaking persons *can* be achieved. Even a "professional" would do well to beware of being too professional. "Stereotyped kindness" will *not* get through. I have the word of an authority on that. Mrs. Mavis Smith, whom I've often mentioned, is more than merely the supervisor of Heritage. She is a professional registered nurse with above-average training, experience, and skill in her field of work. In one of our discussions she said, "Rosalie, stereotyped nursing is not the answer to the needs of those in nursing homes." What she was saying in effect was, "There has to be the human touch."

The human touch, guided by God's hand, is what I try to be to the people at Heritage Manor. I'm called "Teacher," but my real work has little to do with teaching. The time I spend standing before them on Wednesday mornings to teach is seldom ever longer than fifteen minutes.

But the actual work I do is almost full-time—the part which could rightly be called the human touch, guided by God's hand.

There was the man who angrily stormed at me, "I know I'm going to hell," who later wept as I read God's Word to him. I like to remember the lady whose first words to me were, "I'm praying every day to die." I pled with her to pray for her children and grandchildren instead. Afterward, for as long as she lived, she discussed her family with me and asked that I join her in prayer for them.

It was God's guidance, through the human touch, that enabled me to help another lady find peace. She said, "I'm dying and do not feel the assurance that I'm going to heaven."

That was what enabled me to be at Mrs. Lillie Fowler's side when she got the news that her son had died and to go to Mrs. Burns as soon as I learned of her husband's death.

Only God could have kept me from giving up in my effort to provide the comfort of the human touch to one little lady. She couldn't remember ever having heard anyone say they loved her. She was bitter and hostile every time she saw me. Then one day, knowing nothing else to do, I said in a completely meaningless tone of voice (remember, I am *not* professional), "I *love* you!" God must have been in my unprofessional outburst because I never saw a sweeter look of surprise than the one which spread over her face then.

Now, she never fails to smile and say, "I love you the *best!*"

The right kind of human touch is something that's synonymous with compassion. And it has a tremendous force. It impels me to go: to a lady whose son's wife was killed a few minutes earlier while crossing a railroad track, to an employee whose heart was breaking because divorce was crossing the threshold of her home, to a nurse whose husband had just been informed he had cancer of the throat.

Some of the most thrilling examples I've seen of the boundless reach of human compassion have been cases of residents ministering to other residents. Mrs. Irene Cox's home burned with her in it. She almost burned to death. When she was released from the hospital, her daughters brought her to the Home just a few weeks after I began my work there.

Seemingly, there was no hope for any measure of rehabilitation. But one day a few months later Mr. Middlebrooks said, "Mrs. Cox, shake hands with Mrs. Alderman." I stared in disbelief as she smiled and did as he'd asked her to. He had worked untiringly with her, refusing to give up. Her daughters, Mrs. Joanne Lively and Mrs. Betty Sue Lee, still do their part by visiting her. I don't believe a week goes by that they don't come from miles away to see her.

She's still unable to speak at all. She can make sounds, but they're inarticulate. I was sitting beside her one morning during the congregational singing and noticed that she was not being quiet. I looked toward her, meaning to try to get her to be quiet, and saw that she was looking straight at Dorcas and *trying* to sing. I don't know when I have ever been more deeply moved. To human ears, the sounds may have been without tone; but I have an idea that God's ears never heard sweeter music.

She had seemed hopeless. But Mr. Middlebrooks' work with her, her daughters' never-failing love and regular visits, and God's always-ready help made the difference.

She communicated with me once in a manner which is so sweet I like to remember it. About midway through a teaching session one day, she got up from her chair and walked to where I stood and just looked at me. At first, she smiled as if she expected I'd know just what I should say to her. When I made the mistake of assuming she'd merely gotten restless or something and asked her if I might go with her back to where she'd sat, she looked sad.

It was then I realized there was something she desperately wanted me to tell her. I stand in awe of what happened then. (It happens *every* time I'm helpless and at a loss as to what to do or say.)

I'd looked into her sad face but for a brief moment, when I knew as surely as if an angel from heaven had told me—which is what I believe happened—what she wanted.

Mr. Middlebrooks had been in the hospital for several weeks. She wanted to hear from him. I smiled and said, "Honey, I'm sorry I didn't understand what you wanted. You want to hear from Mr. Middlebrooks. Don't you?" She smiled her answer. "He is better," I told her, "and will soon be back with all of you." Upon hearing that, she went straight back to her seat and looked attentively at me until I'd finished.

There is no greater mistake one can make while working with ill people than to assume that those who cannot talk don't know what's going on.

Mr. Charlie Still could and did talk, and it was a joy to visit with him. He was the first one in the home I ministered to individually, except for the lady who was dying and afraid she wasn't going to heaven.

His wife, also a resident at Heritage, died just a few days after I began my work. I went to see him quite often and visited with him for long periods of time. He enjoyed telling me about Mrs. Still and showing me her picture.

During this time he became very special to me, as is always the case when one has a sorrow. But I never heard him call my name and naturally thought he didn't remember it. The manner in which I learned how mistaken I was is one of the pleasant memories I have.

He got sick and was in the hospital several days during which I visited him. Each time I entered his room I'd say, "Mr. Still, this is Teacher."

Several days later, when I said that to him, a nurse standing beside him asked him, "Mr. Still, who is the lady?" I was sorry she asked, fearing he would be embarrassed. (I surely am when I can't remember a name.) But I needn't have worried about *him.*

He immediately answered her, "That's Mrs. Alderman. She teaches a Bible class every Wednesday out at Heritage Manor Nursing Home."

"Mr. Still!" I said, "I didn't know you knew my name."

"I know you didn't," he smiled.

He has gone now to join his wife and is one of the countless throng I'll miss until we are reunited in heaven.

18
My "Errand"

I have one memory I'd like to erase.

Just as I'd entered Branch Manor one day, meaning to check on Mrs. Wicker—Mrs. Revis' mother—Mr. Miles LaHa stopped me to ask if I'd brought the bulletins. (I take bulletins each week to that nursing home too.) I had started to shake Mr. Cleveland Brewer's hand when Mr. LaHa diverted my attention. He talked longer than I'd expected him to, after which I thoughtlessly forgot about Mr. Brewer and walked on down to Mrs. Wicker's room.

When I came back up the hall, Mr. Brewer was crying and asked, "Why are you mad at me?" I was shocked beyond words and asked, "Mr. Brewer, what on earth do you mean? I couldn't possibly be mad at *you* about anything. I love you too much."

"You *are* mad at me," he said. "I had reached out to shake your hand a while ago, and you just went on by."

I remember then that he really had looked in my direction just before Mr. LaHa spoke to me and knew he was telling the truth. Regardless of anything I could say, he continued to weep. For several minutes it was a distressing time. Then I remembered how pleased he had been in the past when I'd talk to him about his wife who is at Heritage Manor.

"Mr. Brewer," I said, "I have visited your wife several times."

He stopped weeping then and asked, "How is she?"

"Not too well. Thankfully, though, she does not suffer."

"Will you tell her hello for me?"

"I surely will," I promised.

As I was leaving he smiled and said, "Thank you for speaking to me." I returned home then, more aware of just how careful I should be when visiting where there are several who know me. To know I made a lonely and ill ninety-year-old person cry is not something I like to remember. I can only hope I'll profit from the bad experience.

I profited a lot from another experience. It wasn't exactly a bad one, but it was so embarrassing that I'll never forget it.

Mr. Gold Russaw asked me one day if I'd do an errand for him when I went back through town. Without asking what the "errand" was I said, "Yes, Mr. Russaw. I'll be glad to. What is it you want?"

"Some chewing tobacco."

"Oh," I said and left, wondering what I was to do. I knew I wasn't going into a store and buy any chewing tobacco, but I also knew I couldn't go back on a promise.

The more I thought about it the worse I felt. I knew there'd be no use asking Edwin to get the stuff for me. He does countless favors for me that are connected with that work, but to have asked him to do that would have been just too much. Neither he nor I use tobacco in any form, and I knew he'd be as embarrassed as I to go into a store and ask for chewing tobacco.

Mrs. Mattie Cooper, who works for me, saw my distress and offered a solution to my problem. She said she'd do the errand for me. When the time came, however, for her to actually do it, she found that *she* had a problem. Neither she nor her son Lucious use tobacco in any way either, and she didn't want to buy it.

Finally, she told Lucious to go and get it.

"Chewing tobacco! Mama! What do you want with that stuff?"

She explained. We both still laugh about it, but I'll never promise to do another errand without first finding out what it is.

That's not to say I've learned everything.

That fact came home to me when I took Mrs. Mittie Kelton riding for the first time. First I took her to my home and showed her through it, then to the farm, several miles out of town. She loved looking at the garden. The cattle fascinated her, and so did the forty or more ducks swimming about on the pond.

On the way back she handed me a dollar. I thanked her, thinking it was for the Bible-a-Month Club, as she is a liberal contributor. "No!" she said. "It's *not* for Bibles. It's for *you!*"

Not wanting to upset her, I said no more until I returned her to Heritage and she'd gone on to her room. Then I told the nurse in charge about her giving me the money and asked what I should do. She suggested that I let her put it back into Mrs. Kelton's purse. That's what I did. It's what I'd do if it were to do over, as I would not, under any circumstance, accept money as a personal gift.

The next time I took her for an outing, I hope I handled things more wisely. That time, when she started to open her purse, I put my hand on her arm, smiled at her, and said, "I want to ask you something. Do you know just exactly why I took you riding?"

She looked at me, her pretty brown eyes sparkling, and smiled but said nothing.

Then I touched her arm again lightly and said, "I love you. Your pleasure at being out is all the pay I want."

Again she smiled. Then she said, "I surely *did* like it!"

She went on to the front door of the home, and I left thinking to myself as I drove on home that I'd spoken truthfully when I told her I loved her.

While on the drive, I'd told her I enjoyed having her as one of my Heritage friends. She asked, "I just want to know what I do for *you.*"

I had truthfully answered, "You love me. You smile every time you see me. *That* means a great deal to me."

She believed me.

The trust Mrs. Kelton and the others have in me isn't something that was handed me on a platter. On that day in May 1969 when I first went out to meet them, they hardly gave me the time of day.

I was back, though, the following morning to stand before them with a message which had even startled *me* as I'd realized the truths I was going to tell them. (Never would I have *dreamed* of standing up in a group of people, most of whom were old enough to be my parents, and saying, "God has not nor will he retire you until your last breath is drawn.")

What must have been their thoughts as I stood up?

19
God Sends Me . . . and You

Mr. Crews probably voiced the question present in each mind when he demanded, "Who sent *you* out here?"

The answer I gave, "God," is the same answer anyone who would work for God and for humanity must be able to give—whether the task is establishing a much-needed *continuing* work in a nursing home or going forth into another day of trying to make an honest living in a highly competitive society.

After I answered Mr. Crews as I did, a quiet stillness fell upon the group. And they listened to me. But my work was not yet done. As far as they knew at the time, I was only going to be someone they would see on Wednesday mornings.

The once-a-week visits of the pianist, song leader, and secretary work just fine. However, the work of the teacher-friend, the one who would put it all together and keep it going, cannot be done during a once-a-week visit. It's very similar to the work the pastor of a church does. He goes to the members of his "flock" at any time he is called.

When I first went out to Heritage, Mrs. Pauline Frazier told me of her concern for "the lady who is dying and is afraid she is not going to heaven." That was ample reason for me to go out there every day, which is what I did until she assured me she was at peace with our Lord.

Then Mrs. Still died suddenly, and I continued going in an effort to help Mr. Still.

About that time I began hearing the residents say to one another, "Be quiet! Teacher's here!" It was also about that time that I realized my work was full-time—there would *always* be a special need of one kind or another.

They began then to trust me as the real friend who was always either there or as close as the telephone.

They also began to love me, as I loved them. That brings to my mind something I feel very strongly about. I shall call it my advice to readers who may be called into a work such as this. Beware lest those you befriend and work with become teacher-worshipers rather than lovers of God. That's something that just won't do. I had the problem for a while and didn't even know it until I accidentally overheard something.

I overheard Vera Thomason, a friend of mine and a daughter of Mrs. Fowler's, telling something Brother Trussell had said to her. He had been out of town when her brother died and didn't get in until late the following night. He'd called to ask if he could be of any help to them.

"I told him," Vera said, "that Rosalie was out there (at Heritage) to help us when we told Mother about the death." She smiled then and told what Brother Trussell had said.

"I'm *jealous* of her!" he'd said jokingly. "When I was going out there every week to teach those folks while she was in the hospital, I'd shake their hands after the service and tell them I'd be back the next week. But *they* would only ask, 'When is Mrs. *Alderman* coming back?' "

I got a hearty laugh out of hearing what he said.

But it didn't remain a laughing matter. Later, when I told Rose Luck about the incident, I realized just how uncomical it was.

She said, "I already know how some of the folks do when you aren't there. They refuse to attend the meeting."

That was *very* unamusing to me.

"Rose," I asked "are you *sure?*"

"Rosalie," she answered, "When you went to Alabama to be with Linda when Mark Edwin was born, you know I taught for you. I helped a lady into her chair. She looked around and asked, 'Is Mrs. Alderman here?' When I said you were not, she asked me, 'Then will you take me back to my room?' "

I was aghast.

The feeling returns as I recall it. I apologized to Rose and will always feel apologetic about it.

Many kind words are said to me and about me as I try to do that work, but there is no danger whatsoever in my *ever* feeling "exalted above measure." The memory of that incident and my experience in trying to solve the problem is sufficient to keep my feet on the ground.

There will always be a tinge of sorrow when I think of the lady who asked Rose to help her back to her room. I failed to get her to change. She loved me dearly but didn't love God enough.

There could be no worse failure in Christian work than for one to love the Christian worker more than the Christ for whom he works. I like to remember how "The two disciples heard him (John the Baptist) speak, and they followed Jesus."

In my thinking, no greater honor could come to anyone than for it to be said truthfully of him, "They heard him, and followed Jesus."

To me there is no comfort in the cliche, "You win some and lose some." I did not win her, and I'll always know that I failed her.

There was another little lady, Mrs. Lucy Johnson, who wouldn't attend meetings unless I was there. My experience with her had a happy ending, however.

I met Mrs. Johnson the day I went out for the first time, just to meet the folks. For a while that day I had a really nice visit with her and her roommate Mrs. Ethel Taylor. An instant love sprang up between the three of us. Then Mrs. Johnson learned I was a Southern Baptist.

She tried to hold back her tears but couldn't. She was that disappointed at learning I was not a member of her church.

"Mrs. Johnson," I said, "don't worry about that. Just remember you and I love the same Lord and are going to the same heaven."

She looked at me with sorrow—she didn't have the assurance that I'd ever get to heaven. Her eyes said so very plainly. Her love for me was so genuine, however, that she promised to attend the meeting the next day.

She did so and never again worried about my soul's security. The Holy Spirit was present in the meeting that morning; and when that's the case, problems just disappear. Quite soon there was between us a friendship which was rare, sweet, and beautiful.

When I first talked to her after learning she just stayed in her room if anyone other than "Teacher" was teaching, I didn't get anywhere very fast. Not until I got real plain with her.

"Mrs. Johnson," I said, "if you won't listen to other teachers talk about our Lord, it means I've failed as a teacher." She protested, but I was adamant. "Yes I *am* right too! I *have* failed you as a teacher *and* as a friend if I'm the only teacher you'll listen to."

She was dear, sweet, sensitive, and intelligent. And she trusted me enough to really listen to my reasoning.

A little later it was my happy privilege to hear her say, when I returned after being in the hospital awhile, "I didn't miss a meeting!" It's a sweet and precious memory, but there will always be a feeling of sadness as I recall the one I could not help in this way.

I try to put the sadness aside, though, and strive the harder to be a teacher whom they'll hear and who they'll follow *toward Jesus*.

One day at the nursing home I was carrying some copies of the *Adult Leadership* magazine in which was a story I'd written about the work done by the folks at Heritage Manor.

Mrs. Linda Hubbard, an employee, saw the magazines and exclaimed, "Is this *our story*?"

As I nodded yes, she was doing two things simultaneously—reaching for one of the magazines and asking, "May I read it?"

Before I could answer her, she had taken the magazine and was gone, clear out of sight.

I still smile as I reflect on her question, "Is this *our story*?"

In a limited sense, this is my story.

But the Heritage Manor residents and their families, the staff members, and the employees can much more truthfully say, "This is *our story*."

It's a story of men and women refusing to become a vast and barren wasteland of humanity, waiting only to die.

It's the story of a fine group of people meeting the challenge to sing the Lord's song in their strange lands.

It's a story of people believing that God does indeed have some kind of work for everyone to do until the last breath is drawn—the retired person, the man or woman in a wheelchair, the blind person, even the one with only a few more days to live.

It can *become* the story of nursing homes everywhere.